S. ELEMENT

Endpapers: Tiny red
blood cells enlarged by a
microscope. A pinprick of
blood contains about 5
million of them.

JUNIOR BODY MACHINE
How the human body works

Christiaan Barnard
Consulting Editor

KESTREL BOOKS

KESTREL BOOKS
Published by Penguin Books Ltd
Harmondsworth, Middlesex, England

Copyright © 1983 Multimedia Publications (UK) Ltd

This book was devised and produced by
Multimedia Publications (UK) Ltd

Editorial: Adrian Sington, Christopher Fagg
Production: Arnon Orbach
Consultant: Professor J.M. Tanner M.D.,
D.Sc., F.R.C.P., F.R.C.Psych.
Artists: Tony Payne, Michael Saunders

First published in 1983

Typeset by TNR Productions, London
Printed in Spain by Printer Barcelona
D.L.B. 31139-1983

British Library Cataloguing in Publication Data
Barnard, Christiaan
Junior Body Machine
1. Human physiology – Juvenile literature
I. Title
612   QP37
ISBN 0-7226-5829-X

PHOTOGRAPHIC ACKNOWLEDGEMENTS
All Sport 42, 85 bottom; Colorsport 50; Daily Telegraph Colour Library 11 left, 12
top, 32 bottom, 77 bottom, 87 left, right; Illustrated London News Picture Library
45; Kobal Collection 59, 61; London Scientific Fotos 43 bottom, 57; Multimedia
Publications 13 top, 35 bottom, 48 top, 49, 56, 62-3, 63 far left, top left, 65, 71
bottom, 80; National Portrait Gallery 34 top; Rex Features 20 bottom, 22, 26 top,
28, 31, 35 top, 38, 40 top, 41, 55 top, 60 top, 63 left, 68, 70, 72, 75, 82 left, 83 right,
bottom right, bottom left, 90; Royal Shakespeare Company 74; Vision International
endpapers, 9, 10,11 right, bottom, 12 left, 13 bottom, 15, 16, 17, 18, 20 top, 21, 24, 26
bottom, 27, 32 top, 36, 37, 39, 40 bottom, 44, 46, 47, 48, 51, 52, 55 bottom, 62 right,
63 far bottom right, top right, 64, 67, 69, 71 top, 73, 76 left, 77 top left, right, 80, 81,
83 left, top, 84. 85 top, 86, 87 top, 89; Zefa 60 bottom.

Contents

Introduction
by Christiaan Barnard

An estimated 3 000 million human beings inhabit the earth,
yet not one exactly duplicates another. One of the most
remarkable features of the human body is its individuality of
appearance.

In a book of this sort, however, it is necessary, briefly, to set
this miracle aside, so that we can concentrate on the biological
principles that make all our bodies work. The field has been
narrowed down, because this book deals with the Junior Body
Machine – the child's body and how it works. A grown-up's
body works in a similar way, of course, but there are
significant differences. A child's body is not fully grown, and
many bits of the body will change dramatically by the time the
body is fully grown. It learns more quickly, but then it has lots
more to learn. Because of this, the Junior Body Machine must
be looked after and protected so that it can grow up with its
full quota of knowledge. This book will help towards this aim.

The concept of the human body as a machine might seem to
be at odds with the idea that we are all unique. We *are*
unique, yet we have thousands of characteristics in common
with machines. Like the car, we derive energy from a high
octane fuel, and like cars we are developed on assembly lines,
though each of us is a product of a unique assembly line
programmed by the genes, the units of heredity.

In fact the analogy should be turned round. It is the
machine which is like the body. After all, the body came first
and it incorporates all the best patents. Human beings
attempt to make inanimate objects perform like living things –
so it is not surprising that machines built for *Homo sapiens* by
Homo sapiens are built in their image.

Junior Body Machine

▲ The arm of the crane is lifted by the cable pulling on the top end of the bar which is fixed at one end. This is called a simple lever. The power to do this comes from burning fuel in the engine. The child's arm lifts a book, because the muscle shortens or contracts pulling on the lower arm, which is fixed at the elbow. The power to do this comes from fuel burned in the body.

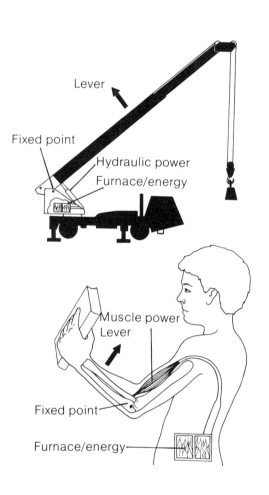

Lever
Fixed point
Hydraulic power
Furnace/energy

Muscle power
Lever
Fixed point
Furnace/energy

Have you ever wondered how your body works? Every day of your life – whether you are sleeping, eating, or running about – your body is working.

The easiest way to understand your body is to think of it as a machine. A machine is any device that does work. Cranes are machines. Their work is lifting heavy weights. All machines need fuel to work, they cannot create energy themselves. A crane's fuel is petrol or diesel. The fuel is burned in the engine. When fuel burns it makes energy, which the engine can use to move the different bits of the crane (see diagram).

Your body is also a machine. It is a machine that never stops doing work, and like all machines your body needs fuel. The fuel is burned in your body's engines – the muscles – to make energy which is used to move bits of your body (see diagram), just like the crane.

Of course, a child's body – a junior body machine – is very different from an adult's body. It is newer and harder to break, it is smaller, it learns more quickly,

◆ Being young isn't just about learning from your elders. Here it is the young teaching the old. The boy is talking excitedly to his grandmother about his aeroplane.

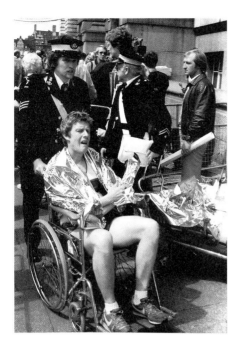

Egg-and-Spoon Race versus the Marathon
Every body machine has a natural limit. If you push the machine over the limit, it breaks down. Some people can run marathons, most cannot. It is no better to run a marathon than it is to run an egg-and-spoon race (especially if your machine breaks down). I'm sure if you repeated that to this marathon runner he would agree with you.

and in its first 18 years, the young body will change more quickly than at any time after that.

Keeping the Machine Going

All machines need looking after carefully. If the body is properly looked after, less goes wrong and the longer it lasts. When you eat, how long you rest and the amount of exercise you take are important. But it is not always true that the fitter you are the healthier you are. You need to look after your body, but if you take too much time looking after your body there will be no time left to enjoy yourself. Your physical *and* mental states both play a part in keeping you healthy. Keeping the right balance and how you see the world are things that you should think about.

And always remember that eight-year-olds are the world's experts on being eight years old.

◆ This young gymnast trains for eight hours a day to keep her muscles fit. But once a gymnast has to stop performing, and that need only be at 16 years old, muscles become painful. They may even turn to fat, which often makes ex-gymnasts unhappy and confused.

● Poisonous car exhaust fumes. Air does not only have oxygen in it, it contains lots of other gases. Many are poisonous, but provided that there is enough oxygen in a breath of air to satisfy the needs of your body, then the poisonous gases will not harm you. One of the most poisonous gases is carbon monoxide, which comes from car exhaust pipes. Unfortunately children are nearer to car exhausts than grown ups and breathe in much more. So make sure you keep well away.

FACTS
Only about a fifth of the air is oxygen, but that is enough to keep us alive. Underwater divers have found that if they breathe pure oxygen for half an hour before they go underwater, they can hold their breath for 13 minutes.

● All animals, including us, are dependent on plants for oxygen.

NUTS AND BOLTS
The Body's Fuel

Your body machine, like all machines, needs fuel to keep it going. The human body needs two types of fuel: oxygen, which is part of the air that we breathe, and food. Without oxygen your body would not be able to get what it needs from food. How this happens will be explained later on. But first, a question. With so many people in the world breathing in oxygen, why doesn't the oxygen supply run out?

The answer is one of the great tricks of nature. You breathe in oxygen and breathe out a gas called carbon dioxide. All around you there are plants – bushes, trees, pot plants, weeds, slime on the pond, mould, grass. They 'breathe' in your unwanted carbon dioxide and convert it into oxygen which they 'breathe' out. So the supply of oxygen in the air is always being topped up.

What happens when we take in oxygen and food?

Oxygen goes into the lungs and from there, through a thin skin with a system of tiny holes, into the blood. These very thin skins filled with tiny holes are called **membranes** and form the walls of the organs inside you. Food goes down from your mouth into your stomach, where it is turned into a mushy liquid and passes on into your intestines. The intestines are a set of long, bendy tubes below your stomach. As the food passes through them, the tubes squeeze out the goodness of the food into the bloodstream through the membranes (see diagram).

The bloodstream, fuelled with oxygen from the lungs and food from the intestines, goes all over the body carrying food and nourishment to every working piece of the body machine.

If we didn't have these membranes full of holes, there would be no point in eating or breathing, because our bodies would not be able to use the oxygen and food, and we would die.

What are membranes made of? (Answer on page 91.)

▲ Cigarette fumes, car exhausts, air-conditioning units – all waste valuable oxygen. In large cities, like New York, this can cause a shortage of oxygen which makes one feel short of breath.

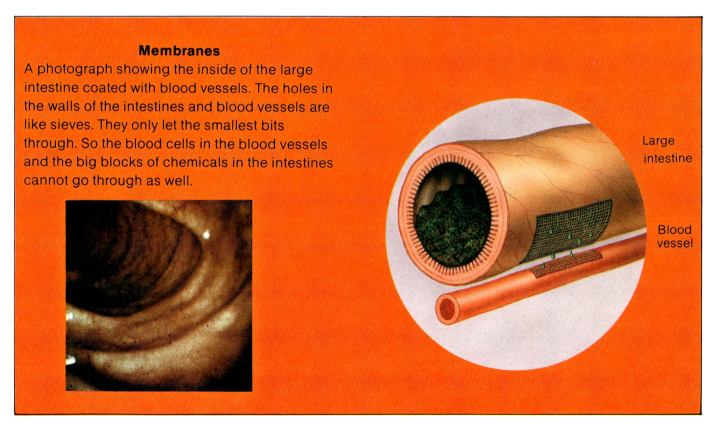

Membranes
A photograph showing the inside of the large intestine coated with blood vessels. The holes in the walls of the intestines and blood vessels are like sieves. They only let the smallest bits through. So the blood cells in the blood vessels and the big blocks of chemicals in the intestines cannot go through as well.

Large intestine

Blood vessel

Breath of Life

Talking

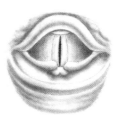

♠ As we breathe out, the air passes through the voice box, or larynx, at the top of the wind pipe in the neck. Inside are two tiny bands of tissue like a stretched balloon – the vocal cords. Muscles stretch the vocal cords, which vibrate when air passes over them, creating a sound. Children's larynxes are small with short vocal cords which produce a high-pitched sound. When a boy's voice 'breaks', at about 14 years old, it is because the larynx, and therefore the vocal cords have grown long enough to produce a low sound.

Breathe in and out every ten seconds five or six times. Imagine if you had to remember to breathe each time. Fortunately it is done for us by parts of the brain we are not conscious of. The brain measures the oxygen level in the blood. If the level is too low, then the **diaphragm** tightens. The diaphragm is a sheet of muscle beneath the lungs which separates the chest from the stomach. When the diaphragm is relaxed it is shaped like an upside-down saucer. When the diaphragm tightens or contracts, it flattens out and the space in the chest gets bigger, allowing air to rush into the lungs. This is called breathing in or inhaling. The diaphragm then relaxes to make an upside-down saucer again, which forces the air out of the lungs. This is called breathing out or exhaling.

When you breathe in, the air rushes through the nose and mouth, down the windpipe or **trachea**, which then divides into two airways called **bronchi** (one bronchus, two bronchi). These then divide into much smaller airways, the **bronchioles**, which open into tiny little bags or sacs called **alveoli** (one

Lungs

Lungs are like sponges. When you breathe in, air rushes in, your lungs fill up like water in a sponge.

Underneath the lobes of the lung lie the alveoli – air sacs – at the end of the bronchioles. The oxygen passes out of them into the blood vessels.

Larynx – the voice box.
The windpipe (trachea) is flexible but strengthened by cartilage rings.

Ribs are attached at the back to the spine, and at the front to the breast bone.

The diaphragm flattens out when you breathe in.

The rib (intercostal) muscles. They contract causing the ribs to swell out making the chest area bigger.

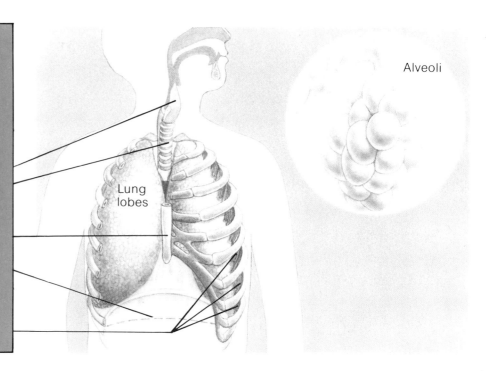

Alveoli

Lung lobes

Sneezing

♦ The hairs in your nose are sticky. They drag out dirt from the air you breathe in and form 'bogeys'. Sometimes dust irritates these hairs causing a sneeze. The air and mucus rush out of the nose – helping to clear it. The fastest recorded sneeze speed is 165.76 km per hour.

FACTS

The lungs are so important that they have to be protected by a cage – the rib-cage. This prevents any weight squashing the lungs.

A sore throat is an illness of the throat caused by invading germs. If it is a bad infection, it may spread down to the voice box making your voice hoarse because the vocal cords are not vibrating freely.

alveolus, two or more alveoli). Scientists estimate there are between 250 and 500 million alveoli in the lungs. If the millions of alveoli in the lungs were flattened out, they would cover an area the size of a tennis court, so the lungs have a huge surface area to take in oxygen.

Each alveolus is surrounded by hundreds of tiny blood vessels. The oxygen passes through the membranes of the alveolus and the blood vessel, into the blood which carries it through the body. Carbon dioxide – part of the used-up air the body has finished with –travels exactly the reverse route through the lungs and out of the body, when it is replaced by oxygen.

Do you breathe as much in the night as in the day?

♦ To play a trumpet or recorder needs a lot of puff. You can get more puff if you push your stomach out at the same time as you breathe in.

What Happens to Food?

Food is used to repair cells and provide energy for them. Before food can do its job, it is converted into a mushy liquid so that it can pass through the walls of the gut into the bloodstream which carries it to the cells. This is called **digestion**.

Digestion starts in the mouth, where spit (also called saliva) is squirted on to the food from under the tongue. The food, now wet and slippery, goes into the gut, which pushes the food along by squeezing – **peristalsis**. The squeezes are so strong that even if you stand on your head, the food can still go through in the right direction.

The food first reaches the stomach. The stomach in the junior body machine is a J-shaped storage tank about 18 cm long filled with strong hydrochloric acid. When you smell food or feel hungry, extra juices squirt into your stomach. If you've ever felt your tummy rumble when you're hungry, that's what is going on. When the food reaches the stomach, it spends two to four hours there as the juices and acid go to work on it. During this time the food is broken down. It is now part liquid and part solid, so that the body can use it.

Leaving the stomach, the food passes into a system of muscular tubes called the **intestines**. These lead from the stomach in two stages, the small intestine and the large intestine. The small intestine is 6.5 m long and is called 'small' because it is narrower than the large intestine. The inside is covered by millions of tiny finger-like projections called **villi**.

In the intestine the mush that has left the stomach is first broken down into a creamy liquid by chemicals squirted into the intestine. Then the liquid is squeezed through the intestine wall, into tiny blood vessels called capillaries which flow around the villi. Nearly all digested food passes into the bloodstream from the small intestine. It can be either used to

Teeth

♠ How many teeth have you got? By the time you are grown up you will have 32. Not all your teeth are the same. The two front teeth are choppers. The teeth on either side are tearers. All the rest are grinders; they grind the food into small bits so the chemicals can attack the bits better. Each tooth is covered with an armour called enamel. This has to be kept clean or it will rot away and your teeth may fall out.

The Stomach

The stomach is an acid bath. The acid comes out of little pockets in the stomach lining. If the acid wears away the lining of the stomach, juices in the stomach start to eat away the stomach wall, causing great pain. Anxiety often causes this to happen, because acid is secreted, even when the stomach is empty.

provide energy (see page 25), or changed into other materials that the body needs. The digested food in the bloodstream which the body has no use for will pass out of the body as a liquid called urine.

The digested food which doesn't enter the bloodstream from the small intestine is in a pulpy form and continues on to the large intestine. The large intestine, which is 1.5 m long gives the pulp one last squeeze to get the water and remaining vitamins out of what's left of the digested food, before passing it out as a solid lump called faeces.

What is your appendix? (Answer on page 91.)

The Digestive System

Oesophagus

Windpipe

Gall bladder

Stomach

Spleen

Liver

Pancreas

Appendix

Small intestine

Large intestine

Rectum

Mouth The teeth chew, and spit makes the food slippery.

Oesophagus Tube that leads from the mouth to the stomach.

Stomach Acid begins to break down proteins and fats.

Pancreatic juices and bile from the gall bladder neutralize any acid in the intestines which may have seeped from the stomach.

Intestine About eight metres long. Most digestion takes place in the small intestine.

♠ Food provides five main types of goodness: fats, carbohydrates, proteins, vitamins and minerals. They are all made of chains of chemicals which can be broken into smaller chains by special chemicals in the body called **enzymes**. Meat and fish provide protein. Bread, sugar and potatoes produce carbohydrates. Milk, eggs and ice cream provide fat. Fats are broken down into fatty acid chains and glycerol chains. Fats are picked up in the lymph system (see page 88). Fatty acids are stored under the skin for warmth and in the muscles for strength. Glycerol is stored in the liver and used for energy. Carbohydrates are turned into glucose chains (sugar) which are stored in the liver for energy. Proteins are turned into amino acid chains which are stored in the liver and muscles, and used for energy and repairing cells.

◆ The liver is the body's central chemical factory. Glucose chains come from the intestines to the liver to be stored. The glucose is converted by the liver into glycogen – a more compact substance – so more can be stored. When glucose is required, the liver converts the glycogen back again.

FACTS
Organs in the body that secrete a liquid for a particular purpose are called **glands**. The liver secretes bile which helps to digest fats in the small intestine. The liver weighs between 1.4 and 1.8 kg, making it the largest gland in the body.

◆ In the desert water must be drunk to replace the water lost through sweating and urinating. Under these hot conditions, the blood reabsorbs as much water as possible from the kidneys, so that the urine contains less water than in normal conditions.

Storage and Waste

We've already seen that digestion produces masses of amino acid and glycerol/glycogen chains. They are carried in the bloodstream to be stored in the liver.

The liver is one of the most important organs in the body. It is a combination of (1) chemical factory, (2) repair plant and (3) storage dump for dangerous substances within the body. When cells need repairing or bones break, the liver releases amino acids and glucose to mend them. It stores precious vitamins the body needs. And it also filters out old blood cells and removes poisonous chemicals and drugs taken in from outside.

Without a liver we would die within 24 hours.

The Kidneys
At all times the body needs a reserve of salty water. This forms the basis of the blood and other bodily fluids, and even the cells which make up bodily tissues (see pages 24 – 25). Many things make you lose water. You lose it sweating and when you breathe out (if you breathe against a cold window you can see the water on the window pane). If you lose too much water, your cells dry out and you die.

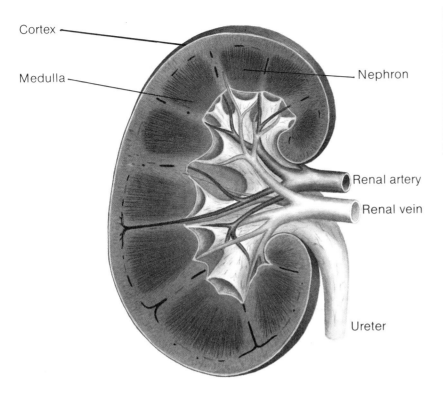

Cortex
Medulla
Nephron
Renal artery
Renal vein
Ureter

◆ Each kidney contains about one million tiny tubes called **nephrons**. Together they filter out waste left over after proteins have been broken down into amino acids. The waste passes down the ureter to the bladder.

FACTS
Fresh, healthy urine is very clean. It contains no bacteria. It is 95 per cent water and 5 per cent urea (the waste from protein breakdown).

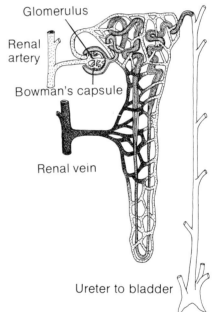

Glomerulus
Renal artery
Bowman's capsule
Renal vein
Ureter to bladder

About half of the liquid lost is replaced by drinking, the rest comes from food. The balance between the water you lose and the water you take in is very delicate, and it is checked by two bean-shaped organs called the kidneys. The kidneys are each about 10 cm long and lie on either side of the spine about half way down.

The level of salty water in the blood passing through the kidneys is checked by the brain. If you have had a lot to drink and there is too much water in the blood, the kidneys take out whatever needs to be got rid of. If there is not enough water, the kidneys take out much less or none at all.

The kidneys also remove waste. The water that has been collected, plus the waste which has been converted into urea, then pass down a system of tubes to the bladder. When the bladder is full of liquid you get a feeling that you want to go to the lavatory. The liquid, known as urine, passes out of you via a tube, called the **urethra**. from the bladder.

What is your bladder? (Answer on page 91.)

◆ The blood passes into the glomerulus (a knot of blood vessels) under such pressure that fluid is forced out of the blood vessel into the capsule. It then passes into the tubule. Here everything that is needed by the body (including 99 per cent of the water) passes back into the blood vessels that are entwined around the tubule. The rest of the liquid in the tubule passes into the ureter to the bladder.

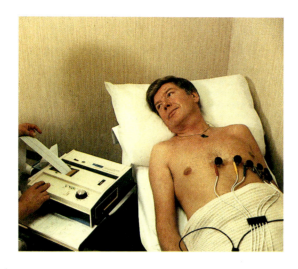

• This man is having an electrocardiogram. An electrocardiograph (ECG) is an instrument for monitoring heartbeat. It can detect disturbances in the rhythm of the heartbeat, and damage to the heart muscle.

FACTS

The heart does not make a bom-bom-bom sound. It sounds more like a lup-dup pause, lup-dup pause. This is the sound of the valves as they open and shut.

The heart circulates the body's blood round the body more than 1000 times a day.

• A heart attack is when your heart stops. It can be started again, but it is difficult. If your heart often goes wrong, doctors can sometimes exchange your heart for a healthier heart taken from a person who has just died, in an accident for example. Heart transplanting, as this is called, is a very long and difficult operation, and it does not always work. But there is a man living in France who is very thankful. He has lived for 14 years with his new heart.

The Body's Pump

The heart is a machine which pumps blood around the body. It has four chambers or rooms. Each of these chambers can contract or clench to pump life-giving blood round the body. There are few machines as strong as the heart. It continues to pump blood throughout your life without stopping – about two and a half thousand million beats in a lifetime.

The heart is a muscle – a very powerful one – at the centre of the body machine. The heart beats about 70 times a minute, sending the blood surging through a system of tubes called the veins and arteries.

The first person to discover how this system worked was an Englishman called William Harvey, who lived about 350 years ago. He discovered that the heart pumps the blood around two different systems. In the first system the blood with no oxygen leaves the heart to pick up oxygen from the lungs. It returns to the heart, and the second system picks up the blood with oxygen and sends it to every part of the body. The blood delivers the oxygen and returns to the heart for more.

Arteries and Veins

Blood is brought back to the heart in veins and leaves

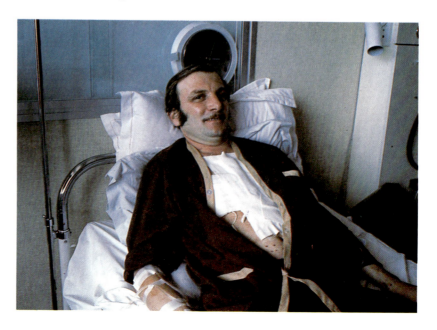

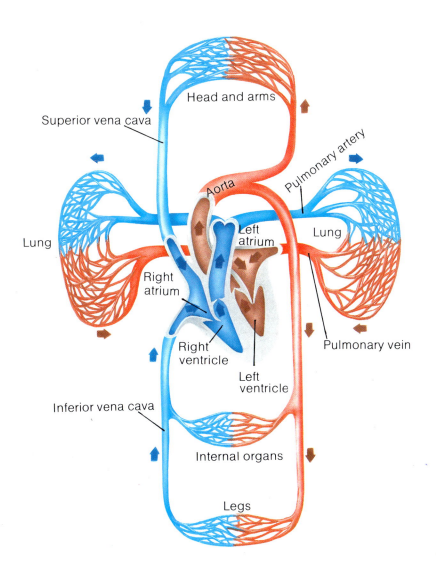

Head and arms

Superior vena cava

Pulmonary artery

Aorta

Left atrium

Lung

Lung

Right atrium

Pulmonary vein

Right ventricle

Left ventricle

Inferior vena cava

Internal organs

Legs

◆ The heart is a muscle divided into four rooms. Each side of the heart has to receive blood and deliver it. The receiving room is known as the **atrium** and the delivering room is the **ventricle**. There are two of each, one on each side of the heart. Each room is separated by a valve so blood cannot flow back into a room once it has left it. Blood returning from organs and limbs without oxygen goes through the heart to the lungs to pick up new oxygen. Then it goes back to the heart before going on to deliver new oxygen to the limbs and organs.

◆ It has been said that when two people in love split up, their hearts break. This is not true. Splitting up can make someone feel anxious or nervous and this can cause the heart to beat faster.

the heart again in arteries. Because blood leaving the heart is being pushed more strongly than blood entering the heart, arteries have thicker, more elastic walls than veins.

You can feel the force of a heart beat quite easily. With your thumb, feel around on the inside of your wrist. Can you feel something beating? This is your pulse – one of the arteries. Count how many times it pulses in a minute. Now try the same with your father's wrist when he is sitting down and your baby sister's wrist. You will find that your father's pulse will be slower than your baby sister's pulse. This is because when you are young you need more oxygen to give you energy to rush about.

How big is your heart? (Answer on page 91.)

⬥ Blood is able to flow upwards through the blood vessels because they have valves which prevent the blood from flowing backwards. But if you stand up for long, then not **enough** blood reaches the brain. The body has a wonderful system to make sure that you get the blood you need. You faint, fall over and as soon as the head comes down to the level of the heart, the blood can flow to the brain again.

⬥ If you cut yourself badly in an accident and lose a lot of blood, it must be replaced by **blood transfusion**. This means that someone else's blood is fed into your veins through a needle. Not everyone's blood is the same and some groups of blood will not mix. Before you receive new blood, you are tested to see what blood group you are. If you have blood group AB, you can receive blood from anyone. If you have group O blood, you can only receive group O blood, but you can give blood to anyone.

What is Blood?

As you now know, the bloodstream is the transport system of the body. It carries water, food, oxygen, poisons, raw materials, waste and everything to do with the way the body works. What is blood?

Blood is made up of millions of red and white blood cells floating in a straw-coloured clear liquid, called **plasma**. Plasma is almost all water. White blood cells defend the body against invasion by germs and against infection after injury (see page 88). They are larger than red blood cells and there are fewer of them. Red blood contains a red chemical substance called **haemoglobin**, which gives blood its colour. Haemoglobin's most important job is to pick up the oxygen that enters the blood from the lungs and to release it to *every* living cell. Without oxygen, cells die. The empty haemoglobin then takes up the cell's unwanted carbon dioxide and other waste and returns it to the lungs.

Normally, muscles receive about one-fifth of the body's blood supply, and the brain one-quarter. But the blood flow to any part of the body can be increased or decreased on orders from the brain. For instance, when you are eating, extra blood flows to the

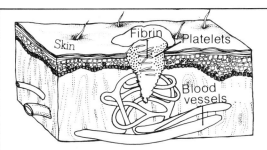

At the moment of injury platelets plug the wound and fibrin threads form a web.

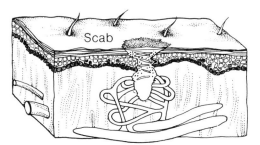

Platelets and blood cells become trapped in the web, forming a plug. The plug dries out forming a scab.

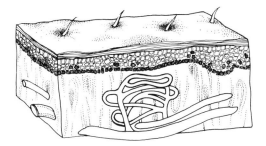

New skin grows beneath the scab. When it has fully formed, the scab falls off.

A red blood cell, enlarged 20 000 times, trapped in the fibrin web, as seen through an electron microscope.

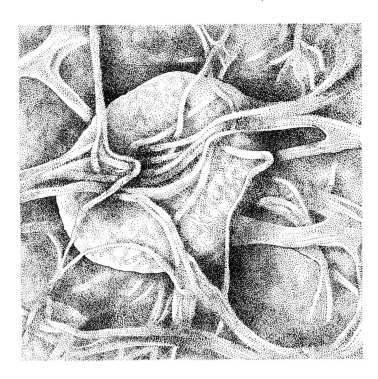

How a Wound Heals

Before the injury, a chemical called fibrinogen circulates in the blood. At the moment of injury platelets, plasma and other chemicals turn the ineffective fibrinogen into fibrin threads. These start to form a web around the wound. Eventually a scab forms to prevent dirt from entering the wound. When the new skin has formed underneath, the scab falls off.

stomach, intestines and liver to carry off the sudden surge of food.

If all the blood vessels of a child could be laid in a straight line, it would be 95,000 km long – a quarter of the distance to the moon. As the red blood cells are driven round this huge system, they rub against the walls of the blood vessels, especially the very tiny capillaries. By the end of 120 days, a cell is worn out by this rubbing and has to be replaced.

The factories which replace these red cells are in the soft centres, or marrows, of the large bones. Each day two thousand million red cells are produced.

How many litres of blood has a newborn baby in its body?

FACTS

Many years ago doctors believed that illness could be cured by cutting a hole in a blood vessel and letting it bleed. The idea was to let all the impurities and poisons out. Robin Hood is supposed to have died in this way.

Ed 'Spike' Howard, an American strongman, donated 500 litres of blood in his lifetime.

50 Million Million Cells

You know that you are made up of different parts: arms, legs, a head, a body. And you know that inside you are other parts – bones and muscles, a digestive system, lungs, a heart and the veins and arteries that carry the bloodstream. But what are all of these parts themselves made up of? The answer is that they are made of tiny building blocks called cells – 50 million million are linked together in one body.

Cells are living things which move and change shape. Like any living thing they need to be fed. Their food is brought by the blood and consists of glucose and amino acid chains.

Cells are divided into different groups that do special work. Each group of cells is known as a **tissue**, and because tissues cannot work on their own, they are grouped together into **organs** – skin, muscle, liver, heart and so on. In every organ, the tissues are packed in a watery substance called **tissue fluid**. This fluid acts as a transport system for the chemicals that come from the blood to feed the cells.

Each cell is like a busy little factory. It is made up of a nucleus, surrounded by fluid contained within a flexible bag or sac. The nucleus contains the instructions for what the cell is supposed to do – to make bone tissue, or skin tissue, or muscle tissue and so on. The nucleus is surrounded by cytoplasm, which contains all the bits which make the cell work (see diagram).

● This beautiful spider's web is covered in drops of dew. The junior body machine is like a web of cells which are held together not by threads, but by a jelly-like substance called connective tissue. The outer layer of skin acts as the overcoat, keeping everything inside.

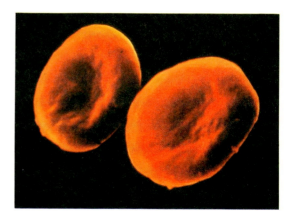

What Happens Inside the Cell?

Chemicals called enzymes decide when amino acids and glucose chains should be broken into small bits. When they are in small bits they can enter the cell and react with the oxygen which has been released into the cell from the blood haemoglobin.

The small bits of glucose and amino acid enter the cell in an orderly fashion. Then some bits go wild and

● Red blood cells are the only cells in the body that have no nucleus. They are shaped like saucers because this is the most effective way for them to carry oxygen and carbon dioxide. It is estimated that one red blood cell makes 40,000 journeys around the body in a month.

Nucleus is the cell's brain. It controls what happens in the cell.

Nucleolus contains a supply of reserve 'food' (protein) for the nucleus.

Endo-plasmic reticulum provides the vital pathway for enzymes moving within the cell.

Lyosomes get rid of any rubbish – bacteria and damaged bits in the cell.

Golgi bodies store protein manu-factured in the cell for use in this or another cell.

Cell wall keeps the cell's shape.

Cytoplasm fills the space between the cell wall and the nucleus. It is mostly water.

Mito-chondria are the power plants of the cell. They contain enzymes that trigger the explosion of glucose and amino acids into energy.

♠ All cells are basically the same. This is a cell about 10,000 times larger than life.

explode with the oxygen in the cell. The explosion creates carbon dioxide, water and energy. The carbon dioxide is waste and is carried off by the blood and breathed out of the body. The water produced replaces the water lost in the reaction. The energy is used for the body's work. Left-over energy is stored to provide warmth, help new cells grow, and feed the enzymes. This reaction takes place every fraction of a second in every cell in the body and is how the body machine works.

How long do cells last? (Answer on page 91.)

FACTS

Cells come in different sizes. Some brain cells are one-2500th of a millimetre long, the female egg cell is ¼ of a millimetre long. To see how small a cell is, peel off one layer of the thick skin of an onion. Under it you will find a thin skin that you can see through. This skin is one cell thick and is the size of a fairly large human cell.

The Body's Frame

Everyone's machine works in the same way, and your insides are the same as your best friend's. Yet no two people look alike, because the size of bones and muscles, the colour and texture of skin differs.

Bones are the body's scaffolding. All our organs are supported by this bony frame, called the **skeleton.** Animals' bones look dry and dead when in the butcher's shop, but living bone is extremely wet (one-third water) and full of activity. It stores all the minerals that the body extracts from food. It also makes the blood cells that the body always needs.

Like the rest of the body, bones are made up of cells. Bone cells are designed for strength and lightness. Bones have to be strong enough to support your body weight yet light enough to let you move around and jump about.

Individual bones are designed for special jobs. Some, like the long bones in your arms and legs, provide support for muscles, others, like the skull, spine and pelvis, protect the organs of the body from damage.

The skull has 29 bones, including your jaw and ear bones. Eight of these are joined together to form the brain's crash helmet – the cranium. The bone is very thin, but it is curved and very strong for its weight.

The skull is supported by the spine. The spine is a column of 26 bones called **vertebrae** that look a little like cotton reels. Each vertebra is linked to the one above and below by rings of gristle or cartilage which act as shock absorbers as you walk. The spine needs to be supported. A support system is provided by thick bands of muscle. The chief jobs of the spine are (1) to act as a protective tunnel for the nerves running down the body from the brain and (2) as a central attachment for the 24 ribs (12 pairs) which form a cage to protect the heart and lungs.

• The brain and sense organs of the head are protected by the skull, whose many bones are joined by jagged joints. The lower jaw moves and is supported by powerful muscles and ligaments.

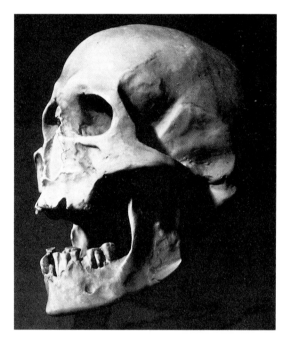

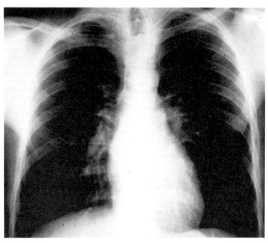

• X-rays allow doctors to see inside the body. They are very helpful, after an accident, in establishing whether or not a patient has broken a bone. This is an X-ray of a healthy rib-cage.

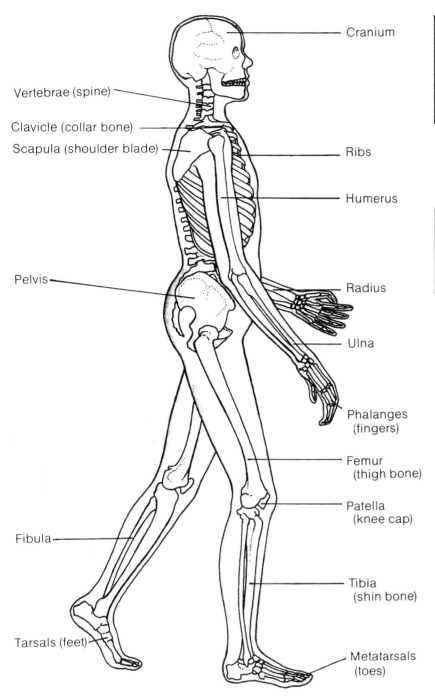

Cranium

Vertebrae (spine)

Clavicle (collar bone)

Scapula (shoulder blade)

Ribs

Humerus

Pelvis

Radius

Ulna

Phalanges (fingers)

Femur (thigh bone)

Patella (knee cap)

Fibula

Tibia (shin bone)

Tarsals (feet)

Metatarsals (toes)

◆ There are 206 bones in the human body. The smallest is the stirrup bone in the ear and is 2.5 mm long. The largest is the femur which is about 50 cm long in a 1.8 m tall man.

FACTS
A newborn baby has about 300 bones, but in time some fuse (join) together, so an adult has 206 bones.

The top end of the spine is held firm by the shoulder girdle. The bottom end is held by the pelvic girdle (your hips). When you sit, almost your entire weight is carried on the flared wings of the pelvis, so it needs to be strong.

The body machine can just about survive without arms and legs but not without its **axial skeleton** –the pelvis, skull and spine.

What is the total weight of an average child's bones?

◆ A baby's bones are made of a rubbery substance called cartilage. This gradually hardens with age, and by twenty-five the bones have finished hardening.

27

Joints

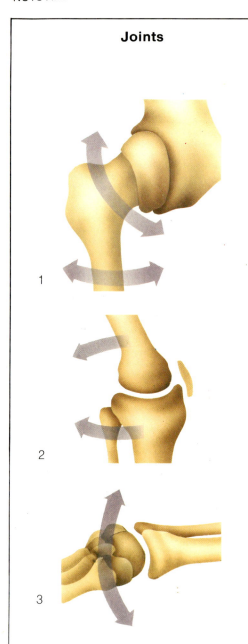

1

2

3

There are several different kinds of joints. Ball and socket joints (1) are found in the hip and shoulder and allow movement in virtually any direction. The socket grips the ball firmly, assisted by ligaments.

Hinge joints (2) allow movement in only one plane as at the elbow, knee, fingers and toes.

Simplest of the freely moving joints are the gliding joints (3). This one is in the wrist, but there are also some in the spine. Movement is restricted by the ligaments.

There are also pivot joints between the top two vertebrae, and these allow the head to turn.

● The thigh bone or **femur** is the strongest and largest bone in the body, because it has to support the weight of the body when running or jumping. The strains placed on bones and joints come from all directions, but the body machine has solved this problem. The femur is a tube which is strong but light. The ends of the bone are filled with a honeycomb of fine bone which is laid out so that from whatever angle the strain comes, the bone will not be crushed.

Levers

The bones in your body are linked together at the joints. Your elbow, wrist, knee and ankle are joints. In all, the body machine has 28 major joints. Joints have to be strong enough to hold the bones in place, but elastic enough to let them move freely. Bend your elbow, wrist or knee and you can see this happening. Notice that they do not move in *every* direction. You can't touch your left elbow with your left hand, for example.

Because the movement of two bones at a joint is so great, there can be a danger of the bone popping out of the joint. Strong bands, or **ligaments**, made from gristle, hold the bone firmly in place.

Of course, if the bones were just jammed together, they would rub on each other as they moved and wear away. The body machine has developed two ways of stopping this happening. First, where the bones meet at a joint, they are covered with a layer of tough cartilage which is slippery and smooth. Secondly, the joints produce their own oil – the **synovial fluid**. If you have ever oiled a squeaky or stiff bicycle wheel, you will know how this works. The synovial fluid gets between the two bones and helps them move more smoothly against each other. When you next cut the leg off a cooked chicken, look out for the white bit at the end of the bone – that's cartilage.

Which is the last bone to stop growing? (Answer on page 91.)

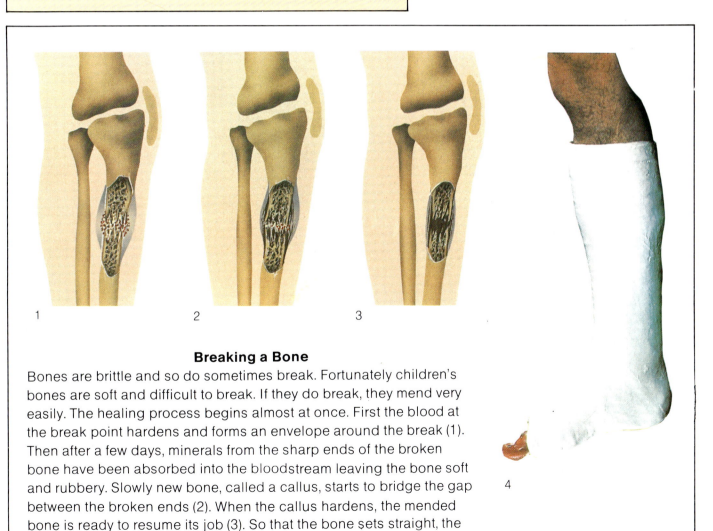

1   2   3   4

Breaking a Bone

Bones are brittle and so do sometimes break. Fortunately children's bones are soft and difficult to break. If they do break, they mend very easily. The healing process begins almost at once. First the blood at the break point hardens and forms an envelope around the break (1). Then after a few days, minerals from the sharp ends of the broken bone have been absorbed into the bloodstream leaving the bone soft and rubbery. Slowly new bone, called a callus, starts to bridge the gap between the broken ends (2). When the callus hardens, the mended bone is ready to resume its job (3). So that the bone sets straight, the limb is protected in a plaster cast for about six weeks (4).

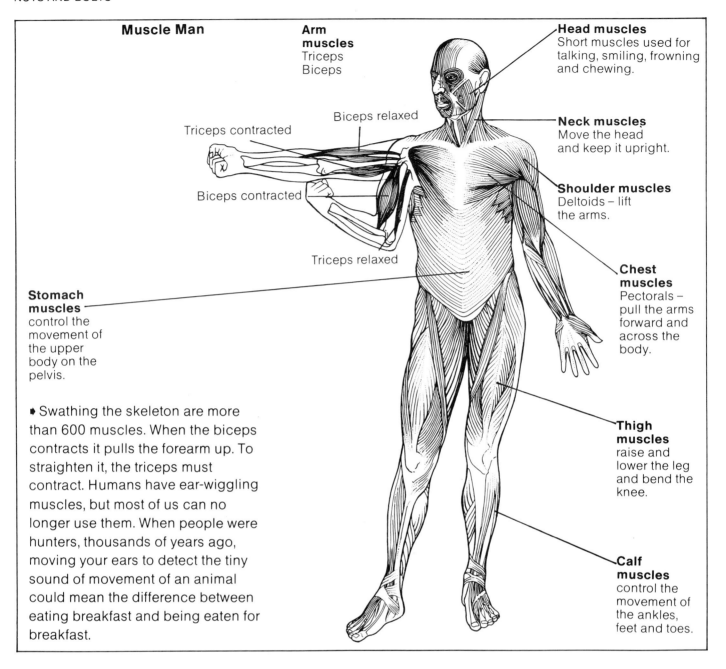

Muscle Man

Arm muscles
Triceps
Biceps

Head muscles
Short muscles used for talking, smiling, frowning and chewing.

Neck muscles
Move the head and keep it upright.

Biceps relaxed

Triceps contracted

Shoulder muscles
Deltoids – lift the arms.

Biceps contracted

Triceps relaxed

Chest muscles
Pectorals – pull the arms forward and across the body.

Stomach muscles
control the movement of the upper body on the pelvis.

◆ Swathing the skeleton are more than 600 muscles. When the biceps contracts it pulls the forearm up. To straighten it, the triceps must contract. Humans have ear-wiggling muscles, but most of us can no longer use them. When people were hunters, thousands of years ago, moving your ears to detect the tiny sound of movement of an animal could mean the difference between eating breakfast and being eaten for breakfast.

Thigh muscles
raise and lower the leg and bend the knee.

Calf muscles
control the movement of the ankles, feet and toes.

Muscle Variety

FACTS
If it wasn't for muscles, our insides would fall out. Sometimes the stomach muscle wall is torn, while lifting heavy objects for instance, and a bit of intestine pokes out. This is called a **hernia**.

You can see tendons in the crook of your arm and behind your knee.

Your body is always moving. Even when you are lying still, your heart continues to beat and the diaphragm moves down and up, first pulling air into your lungs and then driving out the carbon dioxide. Most of the time though, we are moving about – walking, running, talking. All this movement is the work of muscles.

There are two main types of muscle: muscles you can move when you want them to and muscles that work by themselves. Every time you decide to pick up something or walk across a room, you are setting certain muscles in motion. These are the muscles fixed on to the skeleton just under the skin. Other muscles work all the time, automatically, to control movement inside the body – breathing, digestion, blood circulation and so on. Your heart is also made from muscle – a third type of muscle called **cardiac** (which means heart) muscle.

How Do Muscles Work?

Muscle cells convert the energy, which comes from chemicals like glucose, into movement in several stages. Muscles are made of lots of fibres. Muscle fibres can only do one thing – they can only get shorter (contract). When your biceps muscle contracts, your arm bends at the elbow. If the arm only had a biceps muscle, it would stay in that position (if you roll up your sleeve you can see the biceps contracting or bunching). But you have a muscle on the underside of your arm, called the triceps muscle. When the triceps contracts, your arm straightens. So muscles always work in pairs. One muscle moves the bone in one direction, and the other muscle – its pair – moves it back again.

Muscles are able to move bones because they are attached to them by thick ropes of gristle called **tendons**. The biceps muscle is attached by a tendon at the shoulder, at one end, and at the top of the forearm at the other end. When the biceps contracts, the tendon attached to the top of the forearm pulls the forearm up (see diagram).

Like the bones, muscles range in size and shape to suit their job. The smallest muscle in your body is 1mm long in the inner ear (see page 49). Many of the muscles of the face are less than 20mm long. Their arrangement is extremely complicated, and even a faint smile uses about 14 muscles!

Where is your Achilles tendon? (Answer on page 91.)

◆ All muscles are a mass of fibres. When you lift a glass of milk only a few fibres in the muscle need to contract. But when you lift something heavy, every fibre in the muscle will have to contract so you can lift it.

◆ Muscles are always exercising, so that when they are needed, they are warmed up and ready. This constant exercising is called **muscle tone**. If you are nervous, the muscles will have a great deal of muscle tone. You will jump at the slightest noise, like this woman.

● This woman is trying to improve her skin by bathing in mud. The mud removes excess grease and dead skin, and tightens the skin as it dries.

FACTS

Children have about 75,000 hairs on their head.

Hair on the head grows about ¼ mm every day.

Every hair lives two to four years. An eyelash lives about 150 days.

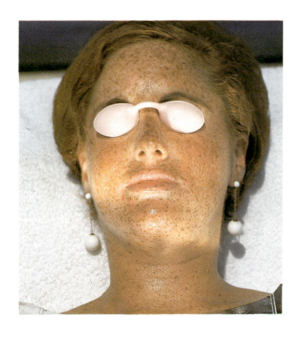

● Have you noticed that your skin gets darker after some time in the sun? Nearly everyone has a substance called **melanin** in the top layer or epidermis of their skin. Melanin gives skin its colour and also protects us from the effects of sun rays, which it absorbs, turning brown in the process. But melanin can only absorb a certain amount, after that we get burned by the sun and start to turn red. White skin contains less melanin than dark brown skins and so burns more easily.

Skin

Your skin is like the wall of a house. It covers the whole body machine in a thin layer of protective armour which holds in all the fragile organs, muscles and blood vessels, and keeps out invading germs.

Skin is waterproof, supple and flexible. If you spend a long time in the bath, the skin on your fingers wrinkles. This is because water has seeped through the tiny holes in the outer waterproof layer, buckling the softer skin cells below. These tiny holes also stop us boiling over. The skin acts as the body's air-conditioning unit. No matter how hot or cold it is outside, the temperature inside the body stays about the same.

Heat is made by the muscles and is spread around the body by the blood. In very hot weather, the blood vessels in the skin get wider. More blood – and so more heat – passes through them and the heat is lost through holes in the skin. At the same time, water passing out in the form of sweat, also cools us down. In cold weather the skin works to retain body heat.

We start to shiver and get goose-pimples. These are produced when muscles make the little hairs on your body stand up to form a cage to keep in the warm air. The tiny movement of muscles when shivering also generates heat.

Like the other organs, the skin is fed by the blood supply from a fine network of blood vessels. The skin is made up of many layers (see diagram). To keep the outer layer of skin tough, new skin is added to the inside to make it thicker. As a result less blood and water reaches the outside layer and it dies. This dead skin forms a hardened layer called **keratin**, which is waterproof. Gradually the dead layers rub off and are replaced by the layer below.

Children's skins are smooth and tight because the cells are tightly packed together, the fibres are more elastic, and because new skin is being added quickly making the outer layer fall off before it gets too hard.

What area would the skin of a nine year old cover if stretched out? (Answer on page 91.)

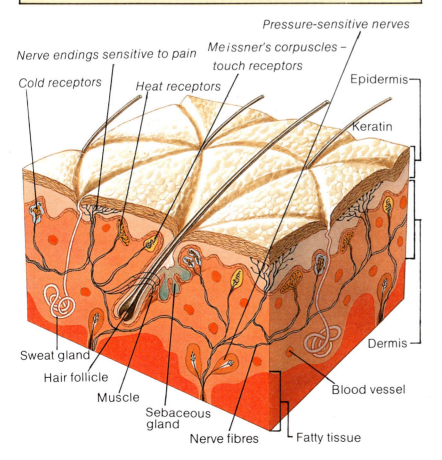

Hair and Nails

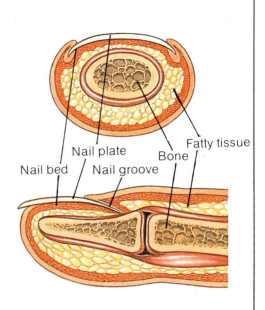

Nail plate · Fatty tissue · Bone · Nail bed · Nail groove

Nails are made of keratin and protect the end of fingers and toes. They are the human version of claws. Hair, also made from keratin, protects us too. Hairs in the nose and ears trap bits of dirt. Eyebrows prevent sweat from the forehead entering the eyes. Hairs on the head and body keep us warm and make us more sensitive to touch. Run your finger along the hairs on your arm without touching the skin and you will feel a tingling sensation.

♦ Skin is made up of three main layers. The top layer, the **epidermis** is like a sieve. it is pierced by hairs and openings for sweat and grease which help keep the skin supple. It contains no blood vessels. The next layer, the **dermis** holds the hairs, grease or sebaceous glands, sweat glands and the nerves which help you feel. Below the dermis is the fat which keeps the heat inside the body. Under the fat is the muscle.

Our Computer

The brain is master of your body, and it controls all your organs, as well as your thoughts and feelings. This is because the brain can store huge amounts of information and because it can deal with many thousands of messages all at the same time.

This is why some people have compared the brain to a computer. But your brain is much more complicated than any computer. A computer never feels happy or sad and it never laughs. Even more important, the brain contains much more subtle information much more useful to you, and much quicker to get at, than any computer. You can remember your name, your address and how to find your way home. You know how to ask for something, you know how to read this book and you know how to ask questions when you don't understand something. You can remember what you did yesterday or where you went on holiday last year. All this is the result of what goes on in your brain.

 Lord Byron, the great English poet, had a large head and a brain weighing 2 kg against an average of 1.4 kg. But don't worry if you have a small head, there is no proof that a large head means greater intelligence and there are many very intelligent people with small brains.

Animal Brains

Brains of a human, monkey, goose and frog. All have the same basic parts. The **cerebrum** is responsible for brain power or intelligence. It seems that the more complicated the outer layer of the cerebrum, the greater the intelligence of the animal. The frog's cerebrum is tiny. If it was chopped out, the frog would survive perfectly well, because it lives mostly by automatic responses which are controlled by the **medulla**. The human brain, however, has a cerebral cortex so complicated that it has bent into deep folds, and without the cerebrum the body machine would break down.

Cerebrum

Cerebellum

Medulla

Thalamus

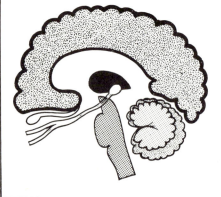
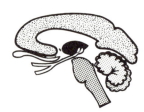

◆ This tiny silicon chip can be used to power a watch or a miniature radio. The brain can be imagined as a very complicated three-dimensional silicon chip. Each cell makes a connection with hundreds of other cells, and if any part of this network is damaged or removed, then the machine will not work properly.

FACTS
When you are born, your brain weighs about 368 g. It then grows incredibly quickly reaching almost its full weight by the age of 7. The brain actually reaches its full weight of 1.35 kg at about 20, after which it loses about 1 g every year.

◆ Firemen have to wear helmets to protect their heads from falling debris. The brain is very easily damaged and in a bad head injury many brain cells are destroyed. This can lead to fits which occur long after the injury has healed.

Nervous Systems

Even the simplest living creatures have a kind of nervous system, to control bodily functions and to tell the creature about the world outside it. Over millions of years the animal nervous system has developed up to the human nervous system which is very complicated, especially in the parts that give information about our surroundings and very accurate control over our limbs. This control, with the ability to work out what is likely to happen next, is called intelligence. We use intelligence to change things in the world in order to help and protect us – to create fire for warmth, to build houses for shelter, to plant seeds for food.

How many nerve cells are there in the brain?

The Body's Phone-lines

♠ When your hair is pulled it hurts. This is because every hair has a bundle of nerves wrapped around it under the skin.

By now you know that many different things are going on in your body at any one time. It is rather like a busy office building. In every office people are hard at work. But they need to be in touch with everybody else in the building so that they know what everybody else is working on. And the building has to be connected to the outside world. That is why a building has telephone lines going out to the world outside, as well as an inside telephone system linking all the offices together. The body machine, too, has a telephone network, called the **nervous system**. Nerves are long pathways, which carry electrical signals. Some nerves make sure that all the parts of the body machine are working properly and in

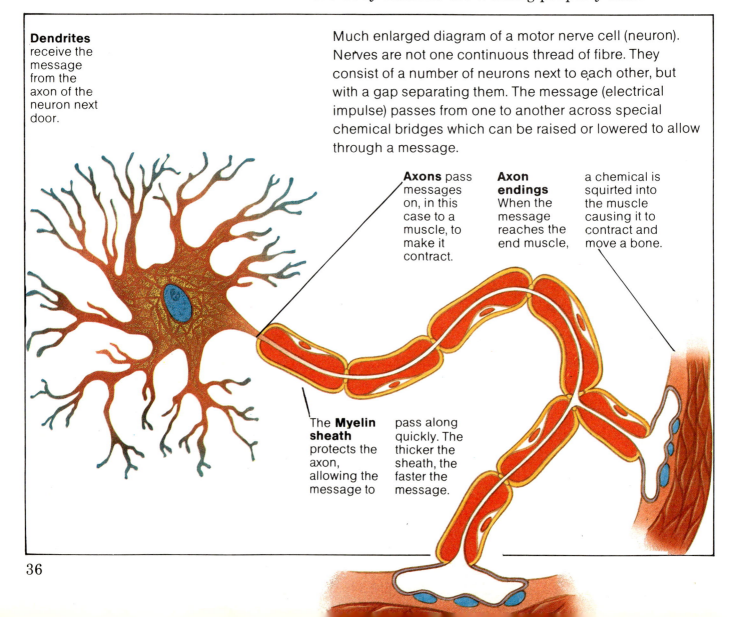

Dendrites receive the message from the axon of the neuron next door.

Much enlarged diagram of a motor nerve cell (neuron). Nerves are not one continuous thread of fibre. They consist of a number of neurons next to each other, but with a gap separating them. The message (electrical impulse) passes from one to another across special chemical bridges which can be raised or lowered to allow through a message.

Axons pass messages on, in this case to a muscle, to make it contract.

Axon endings When the message reaches the end muscle,

a chemical is squirted into the muscle causing it to contract and move a bone.

The **Myelin sheath** protects the axon, allowing the message to pass along quickly. The thicker the sheath, the faster the message.

When you fall over and cut yourself, there is a second between the moment you realize you have hurt yourself and the pain. This is because messages travelling from skin and muscle travel at only 1 metre per second. A message from a punch in the face (or a kiss) takes only 1/50th of a second.

FACTS

Why is a one-year-old child not able to write poetry or do arithmetic? Messages cannot travel along the nerves to the brain unless the path is well-oiled and in young children, the nerve tentacles are rough.

harmony together. Other nerves pick up signals from the outside world – light, sounds, images, smells and tastes. All of these signals go into a central switchboard (the brain). Imagine the brain as a switchboard with telephone lines (the nerves) leading to telephones (nerve cells or endings).

The system is made up of nerve cells, or **neurons** from which nerves reach out to link up with other neurons. Nerve cells vary enormously in size, but they all do the same job – they transmit messages in the form of electrical impulses to, from or inside the brain. There are two different kinds of nerves. **Sensory** nerves transmit messages into the brain. **Motor** nerves transmit messages from the brain.

The junior body machine has a great advantage over a man-made machine. You have to tell a man-made machine what to do and when to do it. The nervous system runs our bodies, without us having to think about it. Heartbeat, digestion, breathing, temperature control – all are controlled by the part of the system called the **autonomic** nervous system.

When your eyes see a flower, nerve cells register the image and telephone a message to the switchboard. The brain then works out what the message means and sends a reply to other telephones in your leg, arm and hand muscles. Your leg bends, your arm stretches out, your fingers hold the flower and your arm pulls. You have picked the flower.

How fast do messages travel along nerves?

NUTS AND BOLTS IN ACTION

Muscles versus Machines

You have now seen all the systems inside the body and how they work. It is now time to see the body machine in action.

You know that a machine is something that does work. Complicated machines, such as cars, need power to drive a system of levers which move the car along the road – this is the car doing work.

The body's power comes from the energy produced when oxygen explodes with useful chemicals in the body. Part of the energy is sent through a system of springs and levers – muscles and bones – to do work. The rest of the energy is used in two ways: (1) to power the internal systems which keep the body going and (2) to respond to the world outside the body through the senses and to react to the information that the brain receives.

How does the body machine compare with other machines? Muscles have been described as the engines of the body. A message travels from the

> **FACTS**
> Shot putters can generate 6 horsepower to hurl a 7.25 kg ball as far as 21 m.
>
> A child usually walks about 19,000 steps a day – about 13 km. Every day its muscles do an amount of work equivalent to lifting 11,000 kg of wheat on to a wagon 1.2 m high.

> ● Muscle pulls muscle. Teams of elderly men from the Basque region of France get together every month for these strenuous tug-of-war contests.

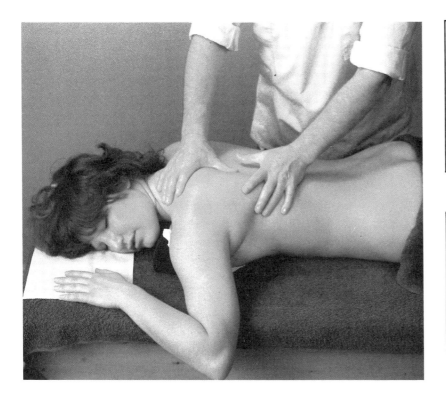

◆ Massage squeezes, taps and strokes skin and muscle. It is an ancient method of keeping fit. And because your muscles are supple after a massage, no energy is wasted moving bits of your body that are creaky and out of shape.

☛ The junior body machine is not very strong. Its muscle fibres are young and thin. It's a bit like the difference between a young tree which is very bendy and a tree, like this one, which is firm and difficult to bend. As you get older, you become stronger.

brain, a chemical is released into the muscle from the nerve-end, causing it to contract. The contraction pulls a bone up or down. How much work can the body do with this mechanism?

A normal 40-year-old man digging a ditch can generate energy equivalent to half a horsepower. This means that in a 40-hour week he can dig a deep ditch 50 metres long. A 20-year-old man could probably dig a ditch about 10 metres longer, while a 60-year-old about 10 metres shorter.

Sometimes the human body can generate up to 6 horsepower, but this is very little compared with the energy a machine can generate. The early cars generated 9 to 10 horsepower and a Concorde jet aeroplane generates 1760 horsepower.

However, the body machine does better in the efficiency race. If everything is working well, up to half the energy produced inside the body can be spent usefully. This compares to only 17 per cent in a steam engine, 30 per cent in a good car and 80 per cent in an electric motor.

But remember it was the brain of the body machine that designed machines in the first place, to make up for its limited strength and stamina.

What is the greatest weight lifted by a human being and the greatest weight lifted by a crane?

39

Muscle Power

The fastest running speed ever recorded by a human being is 43.5 km/h. Compare this with the fastest animal – a cheetah – which can run up to 101 km/h for short distances. Even the big and bulky rhinoceros can run much faster than a human being. Why is it that despite new records set by athletes, there seems to be some upper limit to human performance?

There are two answers to this question. The first is that too much effort would break our bones and tear our muscles. The second answer is that our muscles can only work as fast as they are fed and, in the end, they use up all the fuel that is available to them. In order to understand why this happens, let's take a look at how our muscles use fuel.

Usually, oxygen explodes with glucose in the muscle cells to produce energy. The energy powers the muscles and lets you run, jump and live a normal life. The oxygen is carried to the muscles in the blood. When muscles start to work, the heart pumps the oxygen-rich blood to them more quickly. Remember how the oxygen gets into the blood in the first place. We breathe in oxygen from the air, and the oxygen passes through the lungs into the bloodstream. But

♦ Muscles in the legs and feet of ballerinas have to be extremely strong to withstand the strain of complicated and tiring footwork. Most young ballerinas suffer muscle sprains, torn ligaments and dislocations early in their careers.

FACTS
If the muscles in the body could pull in one direction in one mighty heave, the force would equal 25 tonnes.

The tendons of your muscles can withstand a pull of up to 58 tonnes per square centimetre. They are so strong that bones will usually break before the tendons will tear.

♦ Some people have diseases of the nerves so they cannot use their leg muscles. To get around they have to use a wheelchair. Life in a wheelchair does not mean the end of enjoyable physical activity. Many disabled people train for national and international sporting events with great success. In the recent London marathon some wheelchair entrants completed the 42 km course ahead of the able-bodied runners.

there is a limit to how quickly you can breathe in oxygen, so a different source of energy has to be found. For short periods of 20 or 30 seconds, the body can make energy in another way. Instead of waiting for oxygen to come from the lungs into the blood and then to the muscles, the body can make energy in the muscles themselves *without* oxygen, by splitting up glucose. This takes very little time and the muscles can work twice as quickly. Athletic events such as 100 and 200 metre running races are usually run in this way – marathons are run on lung power.

But muscles need to get oxygen eventually or else they simply stop working and you get painful *cramp*. This is why when you finish a very fast race you puff and pant violently. You are trying to get enough oxygen to all the muscles before cramp sets in.

Perhaps it is a good thing that there are limits to how much work our muscles can do. If they could drive our legs at the same speed as those of an ant, we could run at 150 km/h. But at that speed, the body machine would start to tear itself apart. By working within natural limits, the body machine gives itself the best chance to carry on in the best possible condition for the longest possible time.

When do girls have more muscle than boys?

◆ Few children have the strength to run marathons. Most young runners concentrate on the 100 metre to 1500 metre races. But 12-year-old Kai Bublitz of West Germany has turned in some remarkable times. His best time is around the 2 hour 46 minute mark compared with the world record at senior level of 2 hours 8 minutes. Kai's difficulty is finding time to fit in the 112 kilometre-a-week training runs with his schooling.

◀ This runner is suffering from muscle cramp in the leg. Lack of oxygen to the muscle has caused it to go stiff. The best way to get rid of cramp is to improve the blood supply by massaging the muscle, moving the foot up and down and walking about.

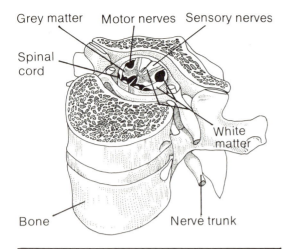

Grey matter Motor nerves Sensory nerves

Spinal cord

White matter

Bone Nerve trunk

• The brain stem is the beginning of the spinal cord which travels the length of the body protected by the bony vertebrae of the spine. Nerve impulses travel to and fro between the cord and the outer reaches of the body along 31 pairs of nerve trunks.

• When the ball is kicked very hard at a goalkeeper from close range, a protective reflex action causes the goalkeeper's muscles to jerk allowing him to save the ball. A signal triggered off a message along a sensory nerve to the spinal cord. Instead of passing the message on to the brain the spinal cord immediately sent a message along a motor nerve which jerked the muscles into action. All this action happened before the brain knew it.

The Brain Again

The brain is the most complicated organ in the body machine. Scientists still do not know exactly how it works. This is partly because it is difficult to get at to examine. The brain is locked into a bone box – the cranium and skull. It is also protected under the bone by three tough membranes and fluid which bathes the brain and stops the brain jiggling about when you run and jump. But perhaps the main reason no scientist has worked out exactly how the brain works is that it is made up of 11,000 million cells, 10 000 million neurons and 1000 million supporting cells. No other part of the body has so many cells doing so many different things. Scientists know which parts of the brain are responsible for certain actions but they are only just beginning to find out how it controls them.

Parts of the Brain

So what do we know about the brain? We know that it is divided into various parts, each of which controls the different ways in which our bodies work. The main parts of the brain are the **brain stem**, which leads off the spinal cord, the **cerebrum**, which fits like a cap over and around the brain stem, and the **cerebellum**, (or 'little brain') which fits into the back of the cerebrum. Life would be much easier if we could point to a particular spot in the brain and say 'This piece here controls the heart'. But we can't. We do know that if a part of the brain is damaged then the part of the body it controls will not work. Every piece of the brain is connected to all the other pieces in so complicated a way that it will be many years, even centuries, before we know how it all works.

What we *can* say is that feelings and hunger and thirst come from the centre of the brain – a part which also runs the automatic mechanisms of the body. The cerebrum – divided into two halves or **hemispheres** –deals with the senses and allows us to learn how to speak and remember. The cerebellum allows us to judge distances and gives us control over our muscles. Without it you would be clumsy.

To carry out all this immense activity, the brain needs an enormous amount of food and oxygen. Only a few seconds' interruption of the blood supply to the brain causes lots of damage, and without oxygen for more than 3 minutes, bits of the brain start to die.

How much electric power does the brain need to operate?

FACTS
The cerebrum is divided into two halves, or hemispheres, joined by a thick cable of nerve fibres. The left half controls the right side of the body. In most people, the left hemisphere is more in control than the right, so most people are right-handed – but not all. In left-handed people, the right hemisphere is more in control.

Inside the brain
A section through the midline of the brain. The brain sends instructions along motor nerves which travel in two ways – (1) down the spinal cord and to the body along 31 pairs of nerve trunks and (2) along 12 pairs of cranial nerves which go direct from the brain to the head, eyes, ears and throat. *Right* Each hemisphere of the cortex is divided into four lobes. By studying the effect of stimulating different parts, scientists have worked out some of the different jobs of some of the parts of the brain.

Areas of control in the cortex

1. Thought
2. Speaking
3. Motor area (sends messages to body concerning movement)
   a) abdomen
   b) thorax (body)
   c) arm
   d) hand
   e) fingers
   f) thumb
   g) neck
   h) tongue
4. Sensory area (receives messages from receptors)
5. Hearing
6. Memory
7. Personality
8. Vision

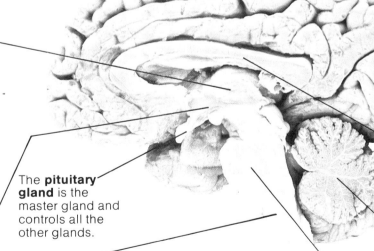

The **cortex** or **cerebrum** makes up 80 per cent of the brain. It consists of two halves or hemispheres of a jelly-like mass of connecting neurons. It is responsible for intelligence, memory, thought and all the processes that you are aware of.

The **thalamus** is the sorting office of the brain. It sorts out the incoming signals and passes each one on to the relevant part of the cortex that will deal with it. It is also the part of the brain where pain is felt.

The **hypo-thalamus** is the link between the hormone and nervous system. It controls the temperature of the body and the salt and water level in the blood.

The **pituitary gland** is the master gland and controls all the other glands.

The **medulla** links the spinal cord to the brain. It controls digestion, heart beat and breathing rate. Because nerves from the spinal cord cross over in the medulla, the left side of the brain controls the right side of the body and vice versa.

The **pons** links the cortex with the cerebellum.

The **corpus callosum** is the mass of nerve fibres (white matter) connecting the two halves of the brain.

The **cerebellum** controls balance and posture, as well as coordination.

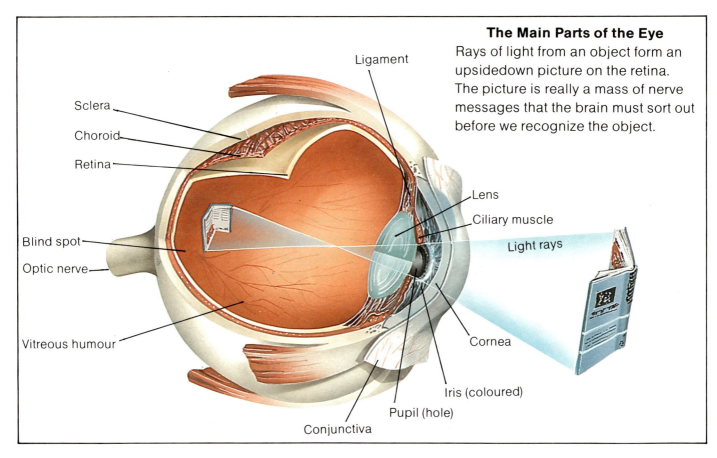

The Main Parts of the Eye
Rays of light from an object form an upsidedown picture on the retina. The picture is really a mass of nerve messages that the brain must sort out before we recognize the object.

Ligament

Sclera

Choroid

Retina

Blind spot

Optic nerve

Vitreous humour

Lens

Ciliary muscle

Light rays

Cornea

Iris (coloured)

Pupil (hole)

Conjunctiva

Eyes and Seeing

• Humans have two lids over each eye. The pink blob in the corner is the remains of our third eyelid. Owls have a third eyelid. You can see it moving across the eye in order to clean it.

To understand what is happening in the world about us, the brain needs to receive information from it.

The brain gets this information from its **sensory receptors**. They are special cells usually grouped together in special organs – eyes, nose, ears, mouth. The skin is also a special sense organ because it contains some of the special cells for touch. The organs themselves do not actually see, smell, hear or taste, they are like a mail service. The letter addressed to the brain is the information which is put into a postbox (sensory receptors in the eye) collected by the postman (sensory nerve) and delivered to the correct address (the brain). The letter is read. Then the brain acts on the information or stores it away.

The most important postbox is the eye. Like a camera, the eye contains a lens to focus the light on to the film or **retina** at the back of the eye, and an **iris** which increases or reduces the amount of light

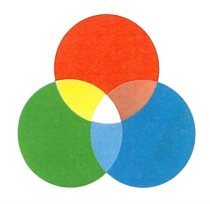

entering the eye through the hole or **pupil**. But the camera is extremely clumsy compared with the eye. Look at the picture on the left. You are seeing a diagram of the inside of an eye looking at this book.

Light bounces off the colours on the page towards your eye. The iris adjusts automatically, like a diaphragm in a camera, to let just the right amount of light enter the eye through the pupil. The lens focuses the light on to the retina. The retina contains receptor cells called **rods** and **cones**.

The rods see things in black and white and are used in dull light. The cones are used in daylight or artificial light and can see three main colours – red, green and blue. The brain mixes all this information together to allow us to see things in colour. We can see 150 to 200 different shades of colour.

Not only can we see things in colour, we can also see them as solid. Because your two eyes are 8 cm apart, each eye sees a slightly different picture. The two pictures are mixed together by the brain in a way that allows you to see depth and to judge how far away things are. This tells us where the body is and helps us make *sense* of the world.

If you stand about 50 cm from a wall and cover one eye with your hand, you will find it difficult to judge how far away the wall is using only one eye.

What is visual purple? (Answer on page 91.)

● The eye contains three types of cone. Each type is sensitive to either red, green or blue light. All the other colours can be produced by mixing together different amounts of these. If you mix red, green and blue together, white light is produced. People with faulty red-sensitive or green-sensitive cones are usually colour blind.

Eyesight

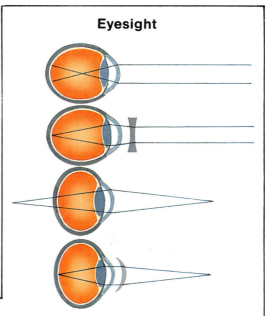

Eyes vary in shape. If the eye is too long, as in short-sighted people, they can focus on nearby objects, but rays from a far-off object come to a focus short of the retina. This means that they will see the object blurred. (The rays have to come to a focus *on* your retina for you to see an object clearly.) If the eye is too short, as in long-sighted people, they can focus on far away objects, but rays from nearby objects come to a focus beyond the retina.

Spectacles, containing convex lenses, which curve outwards (for long sight) or concave lenses, which curve inwards (for short sight), restore normal vision. This is an early pair of spectacles made in 1850 for a short-sighted man.

Smell and Taste

Smell and taste are two senses that work closely together. Many of the things you think you are tasting you are actually smelling. If you hold your nose and shut your eyes you will not be able to taste the difference between an apple and an onion.

By sniffing, you draw the smell of, say, a hamburger, over special receptor cells in the nose which have sticky hairs. The smell dissolves in the sticky liquid and the receptor cells sort out all the different chemicals which go to make up the smell into a form the brain can understand. The information is passed rapidly to the brain which combines the information to give you a sensation of smelling.

Taste works in a similar way. The receptor cells for taste – the taste buds – are on the tongue. Smell is much more sensitive than taste. There are four kinds

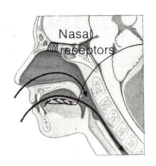

Smelling

The air entering the body through the nose or mouth does not normally pass over the nerves that recognize smell. So we have to sniff to push air up towards them. Hot food gives off molecules that float through the air. These are then sniffed on to the smell receptors which recognize what they are.

◆ A baby feeds from its mother as soon as it is born. At this stage its eyesight is not very good, but a baby can recognize its mother by smell.

FACTS

The average Briton eats more sweets than anyone else in the world.

Each one of us has an individual smell as distinctive as our fingertips.

One of the world's worst smelling substances is ethyl mercapatan: it smells of a combination of rotting cabbage, garlic, onion and sewer gas!

Over 17,000 smells have been officially classified.

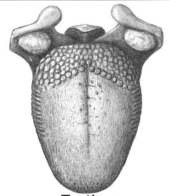

Tasting

The tongue helps in tasting food as well as swallowing and talking. Salty and sweet things are tasted on the tip, bitter things at the back and sour things at the sides of the tongue.

◆ Fresh tuna fish for sale in a Tokyo market. They will smell good, but if they were left for a few days, they would start to smell horrible. Strong smells irritate the sensitive smell receptors causing a stinging sensation and tears.

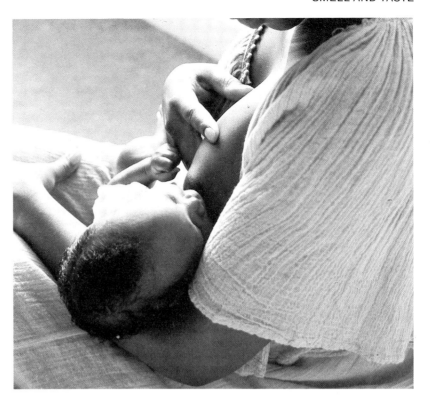

of taste bud. Each one is a clump of cells responding to four different tastes – sweet, sour, salt or bitter. Smell receptors are much more sensitive: they are thought to be sensitive to 15 different kinds of smell. This may not seem a lot, but combined in different ways, it adds up to the 10,000 different smells that human beings can detect.

An adult has 9,000 taste buds which is far fewer than babies. As the body machine gets older, taste gets worse. This may explain why grown-ups never believe children's complaints about foul-tasting medicines!

It is not known what makes one child love mashed potato while another hates it. But it is certain that most children love sweet things.

Babies are born with a preference for sweet things. One explanation is that the body needs sugar for energy. But scientists now think it may be a habit left over from the days when early humans fed on plants and berries. Sweeter ones are usually safe to eat, but bitter ones are often poisonous.

How does our sense of smell compare to that of a dog?

FACTS
Noise is measured in decibels. A whisper registers about 30 decibels. A rifle shot may measure 150 decibels. Loud noises, over 130 decibels, can permanently damage the ears. Sounds over 175 decibels can kill people.

Pressure receptors in the soles of your feet help you to keep your balance.

● All animals have different sounds that they can hear best. Rats can hear high-pitched squeaks that we cannot hear. These are like the sounds made by baby rats, so the mother rat can find its young in the dark.

Ears and Balance

The human ear is perhaps the best-designed organ in the body. Its two main jobs are to allow us to hear and help the body keep its balance. Both are vital in helping the body orientate itself – to know where it is so that it can react to what is going on outside of it.

The ear has three parts – the outer, middle and inner ear. The outer ear is the ear flap which catches and funnels sound into the ear. It is separated from the middle ear by a passage, lined with hairs, which secretes wax to protect the ear from interference, such as insects. At the end of the passage is the eardrum, which seals the passage like a door. When a soundwave hits the drum, it shakes or vibrates. In the middle ear, resting against the other side of the drum is a system of three tiny bones that act as levers making the vibration about 20 times larger. One of the bones rests against the inner ear sending the vibrations to a fluid in the actual organ of hearing. This is called the **organ of Corti**. It is inside the

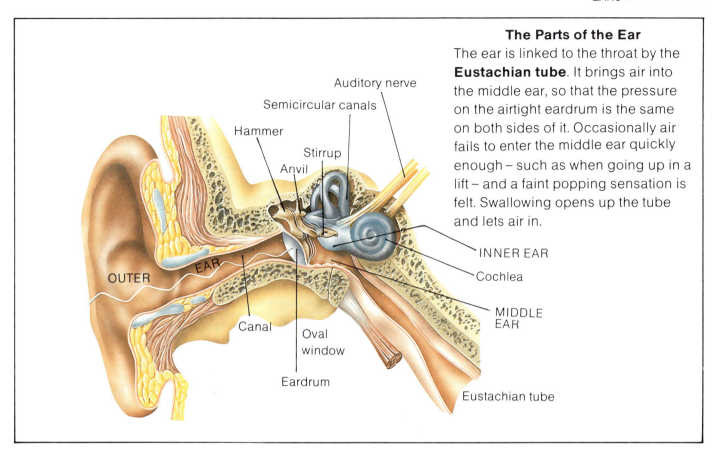

Auditory nerve
Semicircular canals
Hammer
Stirrup
Anvil
OUTER EAR
Canal
Oval window
Eardrum
INNER EAR
Cochlea
MIDDLE EAR
Eustachian tube

The Parts of the Ear

The ear is linked to the throat by the **Eustachian tube**. It brings air into the middle ear, so that the pressure on the airtight eardrum is the same on both sides of it. Occasionally air fails to enter the middle ear quickly enough – such as when going up in a lift – and a faint popping sensation is felt. Swallowing opens up the tube and lets air in.

fluid-filled coil called the **cochlea**. The organ of Corti works like a piano keyboard, except instead of keys it has hair cells.

The vibrating fluid moves along the keyboard pressing the keys (hairs). Higher sounds cause the fluid to press more keys. The brain then registers how many hairs have been pressed and hears a sound.

The human ear can distinguish sounds ranging from the lowest register of an organ (which vibrates 16 times a second, or at 16 hertz) to the high-pitched scraping of a grasshopper (20,000 hertz). Babies and children hear a much greater range of sound than adults. By the age of 60, you will be lucky if you can hear sounds as high as 12,000 hertz. This is because hair cells are gradually lost in the cochlea.

The range of sounds picked up by the human ear is not impressive when compared to other animals. Bats and porpoises can hear frequencies as high as 100,000 hertz.

Why do people put their ears to the ground to listen for the approach of galloping horses? (Answer on page 91.)

◆ This girl can tell the direction from which she is being called. Because our ears are 15 cm apart, sound reaches one ear a fraction of a second before it reaches the other. From this time difference, the brain can plot the direction of the sound.

Touch

Pain

Finally the man is tackled and in a blur of pain he tumbles to the ground. Pain is felt by free nerve endings in the skin. It is thought that these nerve endings can feel all the types of touch that have been described. But they send off a message to the brain only if they are over-stimulated. So if you are shaking hands, then pressure and heat receptors are working. If the shake turns to a squeeze, then the free nerve endings whizz a painful message to the brain. Pain is not the same thing as a hurt or injury. If you burn your finger on a stove it is hurt. Pain is what you feel afterwards in the brain.

Touch is another way we learn about the things that surround us. The sense of touch is the hardest sense to understand, because there is no single organ or postbox to post the letter to the brain.

Get a friend to help you try this experiment. You will need a piece of material (a sweater will do) and a bowl of water. Close your eyes and ask your friend first to hand you the sweater, then to guide your hand into the water. Finally ask your friend to squeeze your hand – not too tight! Can you describe the different sensations you feel?

These three sensations tell you something about the sense of touch. First there is a sense of **texture** – the way the sweater feels in your hand. Secondly there is a sensation of **temperature** – whether the water feels hot or cold (and the fact that it feels wet!). Thirdly there is the sense of **pressure** as your friend squeezes your hand. All three add up to the sense of **touch**. And there is something more. If the texture is too rough, if the water is too hot, or if your hand is squeezed too hard, you will feel *pain*. Touch can also be felt inside the body – hunger, tiredness, tummy ache and so on.

Most touch is experienced through sensory receptors in the skin. Each type of touch is registered by a special receptor. There is not the same number of each type of receptor. There are more pain receptors than any other. Then comes pressure, then heat, and cold. This means that you can say where you feel pain much more precisely than where you feel cold. Different parts of the body are more sensitive than others. That means they have more receptors in a given area. You can test the sensitivity of different parts of the body with two sharpened pencils. Hold the pencils so the points are 5mm apart. Only your fingers, nose and tongue can tell that there are two points. (Be careful of your eyes!) On the

◆ Getting wet can be terrific fun. But can you describe the feeling of wetness? The four basic touch sensations are pressure, coldness, hotness and pain. Wetness is a combination of pressure and coldness – and sometimes pain, if the water is cold!

thighs, the points have to be about 5cm apart before two points are felt. The middle of the tongue is the most sensitive part of the body, the middle of the back, the least.

What does a two centimetre square of skin on the palm of your hand contain? (Answer on page 91.)

FACTS

After a leg has been cut off – amputated – the brain's memory of a limb lingers on, and so the patient may still be able to feel it for some time.

The hottest temperature endured by a person on bare skin was 812°C when walking on specially-prepared white hot coals in Melbourne in 1976.

◆ A baby's instinct to wrap its hand around small objects shows itself at birth. By touching everything around it, a baby soon learns to recognize different things, and whether they are comforting or threatening.

Chemical Messengers

The body machine has chemical messengers called **hormones**. They are controlled by the brain and are responsible for regulating change in the body.

The body machine has a timetable of changes that must happen. A junior body machine should be growing all the time. It should lose its baby teeth at about six. Between the ages of 10 and 15 your muscles develop and your voice changes. All these changes occur because special **glands**, like water pistols, squirt out different hormones which act on the various parts of the body.

There are two types of gland. **Endocrine glands** squirt the hormone into the blood, which carries it to the organ to be activated. The other type – **exocrine glands** – squirt a hormone on to the organ direct, for instance, the salivary gland under the tongue squirts saliva or spit into the mouth to digest food.

● Before facing the bull, bull-fighters in Spain often prepare themselves mentally by praying. At the same time, the body is pumping out the hormone **adrenalin** into the bloodstream. The effect is immediate. Breathing gets faster, bringing in more oxygen, and the heart beats faster, pumping the oxygen around the body at a faster rate. Blood is diverted from the skin and digestive system to the muscles where it is needed most. The extra oxygen means the muscles can fight for longer without tiring. The bull-fighter's hormones have helped him by preparing him for sudden action. Without adrenalin, he would not be able to fight the bull so well and might be killed.

The glands are fired in quite a neat way. A part of the brain called the **hypothalamus** sends a message to the chief gland – the **pituitary** (although nobody knows what makes the hypothalamus decide to do it). The pituitary gland, which is also in the brain, has all kinds of separate compartments, each of which contains a different hormone. Some of the hormones act directly on various organs, such as the bones, kidneys and womb. But most of the hormones are messengers which carry messages to other glands in the body telling them to squirt hormones.

Here is a test for you to see how your salivary gland works. Go into the kitchen and get some of your favourite food from the refrigerator. Look at it. What is happening in your mouth? It is filling up with spit or saliva. This is because the eye saw the food and sent its message to the brain, which, in case you decide to eat it, has told the salivary gland to start squirting the saliva into your mouth.

One of the jobs of the endocrine system is to control how hot you are. This is your body temperature, and it is normally between 35.5 and 37°C. If it drops, blood temperature will also drop. As the cooler blood passes through the brain, the hypothalamus will measure its temperature and send off a message to the pituitary gland, which in turn will send off instructions to different organs of the body to try to keep the temperature normal. This is important because the temperature need only rise or fall by 5°C for the body machine to stop working or die.

Where does the word 'hormone' come from?

FACTS

The pituitary gland is the size of a pea. It hangs from the underside of the brain in a small bone hollow called the Turkish Saddle.

The tallest living giantess lives in Canada. She is 236.7 cm tall. At the age of 13 she was 198 cm tall.

Where Hormones Come From

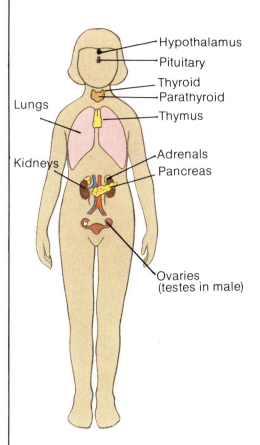

- Hypothalamus
- Pituitary
- Thyroid
- Parathyroid
- Thymus
- Lungs
- Kidneys
- Adrenals
- Pancreas
- Ovaries (testes in male)

The **pituitary gland** controls the thyroid, adrenal and reproductive glands; controls body growth.
The **thyroid gland** controls the rate at which food is converted into energy in the cells.
The **parathyroid gland** controls the level of calcium in the blood.
The **thymus gland** helps to recognize and reject bacteria and germs. Very little is known about how it works.
The **adrenal gland** has two parts, the outer cortex and the inner medulla. The cortex helps to prepare the body when frightened, angry or excited. The medulla helps fight stress and shock.
The **pancreas** controls the body's use of glucose.
The **ovaries** control the growing-up process in girls.
The **testes** control the growing-up process in boys.

The Assembly Line

FACTS

The ovaries of a newborn girl contain all the egg cells she will ever produce – as many as one million. These egg cells rapidly die until there are only 300,000 left at puberty.

The coils and tubes that make up the internal genitals of a mature man would extend 1600 km if unravelled.

Hormones are also responsible for making new body machines. Building a new machine like a car is easy. First you get the frame, add the wheels, cover it with a painted skin and attach an engine. Off you go.

Making a new body machine is much more complicated. For a start you cannot get the parts ready-made and bolt them together. Also you cannot make a new body machine whenever you want.

As you have seen, the body is changed by hormones according to a timetable. It is not until the age of about 16 that the parts needed to make a baby are working. How they do it is complicated.

The first thing to remember is that bodies are made of thousands of millions of cells – your tissues and

The Sex Organs

The male sex organs or genitals lie outside the body. This is because the sperm cannot be produced at normal body temperature which is too high, and so they are made in the testes in a bag – the scrotum – outside the body, where it is a little cooler.

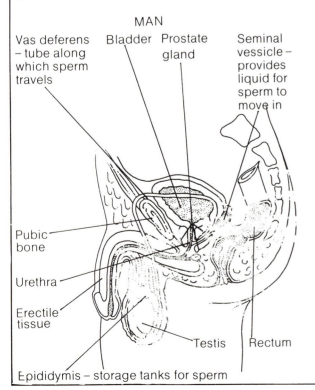

MAN

Vas deferens – tube along which sperm travels

Bladder

Prostate gland

Seminal vessicle – provides liquid for sperm to move in

Pubic bone

Urethra

Erectile tissue

Testis

Rectum

Epididymis – storage tanks for sperm

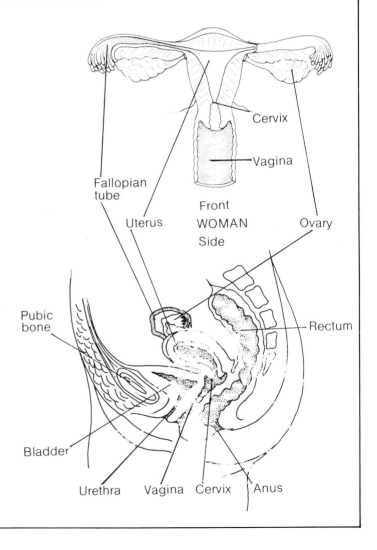

Cervix

Vagina

Fallopian tube

Uterus

Front
WOMAN
Side

Ovary

Pubic bone

Rectum

Bladder

Urethra

Vagina

Cervix

Anus

organs. Men have some special cells which are kept in one place. They are called sperm cells and they live in the testicles, where they are made. The testicles are in the scrotum, which is a bag under the penis. Woman have special cells, too. They are called eggs, which live in the ovaries, which are inside a woman's body.

Only men have sperm, and only women have eggs. For a new baby to be made, a sperm has to join up with an egg to form a fertilized cell, or **zygote**, which must grow. This happens *inside* the woman's body. When this happens the woman is pregnant. All that these special cells have to do is wait until they are joined together. They have no other job until that time.

When does it happen? Men produce sperm all the time, and the sperm are ready to make babies at any time. Because a woman has to carry the developing baby for nine months, the egg and her insides need to be prepared for this task. Hormones control this preparation. It takes hormones about one month to prepare a woman's body to carry a new baby. Each month there is a time when the egg will be ready to be joined by a sperm. But the egg will die and be flushed out of the body – called **menstruation** or having a period – if the sperm has not joined it within two days of the egg being ready.

How does the sperm reach the egg? Men have penises, and women have vaginas. Both are tubes or passageways. The vagina leads to the uterus (womb) where there are two more tubes called **Fallopian tubes**. The egg must be in one of these two tubes if the woman is to become pregnant. When a man and a woman make love, the man's penis becomes stiff and hard and is pushed into the woman's vagina, which has opened up and become slippery. The sperm are then squirted out of the penis into the vagina. About 300 million sperm are produced.

How long is a mature sperm cell? (Answer on page 91.)

● In some parts of Africa living conditions are very hard. Having children is essential to make sure that the group survives in the future. Because it is so important, these men and women from Mali have dressed up and are dancing around to bring them good luck in having children.

● Today large families like this one are comparatively rare in the western world. Family planning, or contraception, to prevent women having more children than they want, was introduced into Europe at the end of the last century. But only in the last 30 years has contraception become widespread.

Making a Baby

So 300 million living, wriggling sperm are in the vagina trying to get to the egg. Of the 300 million only one will make it, and the rest will die within two days. Of course the egg may not be ready to be fertilized, and then the sperm's journey has been wasted. The journey is very long. It is as though a human being had to travel many kilometres in two days. First of all the sperm passes through the cervix, the entrance to the womb. Most sperm will not have made it this far; they will have been killed by the acid in the vaginal area. More sperm will go down the Fallopian tube that doesn't have an egg in it. Between 1,000 and 100,000 will enter the Fallopian tube containing the egg. Finally the sperm reaches the egg. Only 100 or so have survived the journey. At this point one sperm secretes a special chemical which makes a hole in the egg's cell wall. This may take several hours even though the wall is quite thin. Once the sperm starts to penetrate the egg, chemical changes take place preventing any other sperm entering the egg.

In the next few days the fertilized egg will divide six or seven times to form about 150 cells before beginning another journey, down the Fallopian tube to the uterus, where the egg will grow into a baby.

● Identical twins are always the same sex and develop when the fertilized egg splits into two. Fraternal twins are not identical but just as alike as any two children from the same parents. They happen when two eggs are fertilized by two different sperm.

The Growing Foetus

At the ninth week the embryo becomes recognizable as a human being and is known as the foetus. The tail – left over from our fishy ancestors – is now disappearing. The head is forming and all the main internal organs – liver, heart, kidneys and spleen – have developed.

Six weeks later. Only 6 mm long, the embryo is attached to the placenta by the umbilical cord which supplies it with blood.

Fertilization of ovum in Fallopian tube.

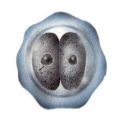

The first cell division 48 hours later.

Morula stage. Embryo enters uterus.

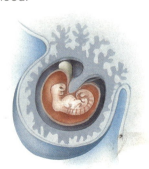

The womb is a life-support system which will supply the fertilized egg with all the food and oxygen it needs to grow into a baby. In the beginning the egg lodges in the soft lining of the uterus – the **placenta** – which is rich in blood vessels. Later, as the baby grows, the attachment turns into a tube –the **umbilical cord** – which carries a supply of blood with oxygen and energy from the mother's body to the growing baby.

If you were able to enter a womb just before birth, after the foetus, as the baby is called, had been in the womb about 280 days, you would see a little body machine floating in what looked like water. One of the miracles of birth is that the body machine lives under water for nine months and then enters the outside world, where within two minutes it is breathing through the mouth, using its lungs.

What is a premature baby? (Answer on page 91.)

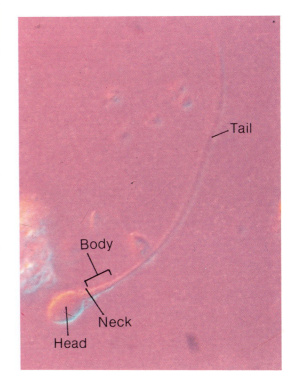

Tail

Body

Neck

Head

● The head of the sperm contains a large nucleus filled with chromosomes. The neck joins the body, which contains mitochondria (see page 25), that provide the power to move the tail which drives the sperm.

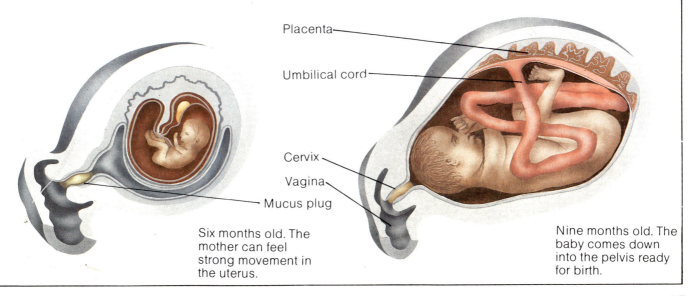

Placenta

Umbilical cord

Cervix

Vagina

Mucus plug

Six months old. The mother can feel strong movement in the uterus.

Nine months old. The baby comes down into the pelvis ready for birth.

How DNA copies itself

Chromosomes have to duplicate themselves to create new cells (see diagram opposite). This is how it is done.

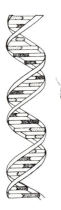

Each chromosome is made up of strands of DNA. The DNA molecule is like a twisted ladder with rungs. The rungs are made of two chemicals called bases joined together. The bases on a DNA molecule can only pair in a certain way.

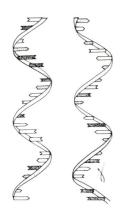

When the two strands separate, they leave the bases bare.

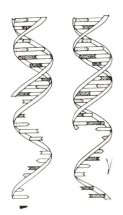

A new matching strand is built up beside each strand.

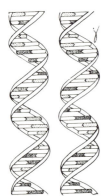

Two new DNA molecules are formed. Both are exactly the same as the original DNA molecule and carry the same instructions (see stage 2 in diagram opposite).

Blueprints

To build any new machine, whether it's a car, radio or washing machine, you need a plan or a blueprint. The same is true of the body. Hormones develop the body machine to the point where it can have children. They even control the time of the month at which a sperm can meet the egg. But at this point the fertilized egg takes over. In the nucleus of the fertilized egg there are chemical codes – **chromosomes** – which are the blueprints for the growing baby.

Every cell in the embryo has the same set of chromosomes. All chromosomes are made up of blocks called **genes**. Genes are made of chemicals called DNA or deoxyribonucleic acid. Like computer tape DNA contains coded instructions. The instructions tell the cell how it should behave. They tell the cells which features of the face, the colour of the eyes and hair to make. Every cell in your body has an identical set of genes, containing *all* the instructions. So, we think that when the eye is being made in the embryo, the eye cells 'read' through the computer tape until it gets to the bit about eye colour and then obeys the instructions.

Every cell in the grown-up body, except for the sex cells, has 46 chromosomes. The sperm and egg cells contain half this number – 23 single chromosomes. When the two cells join together, they make up the full number of 46 chromosomes.

All the cells in your body – except the sex cells –are busy making copies of themselves (see diagram). That's why, although individual cells die, your body can carry on living up to 100 years. Sex cells can only start to reproduce themselves when the sperm and egg get together. Then with their full number of chromosomes the fertilized sex cell begins the long and miraculous task of creating another human being.

What is a mongol child? (Answer on page 91.)

• Tarzan in the jungle. The body machine keeps the same set of chromosomes from birth to death. However, how you grow up is not just controlled by your genes. How, where and who you live with mould your personality as well.

Making Sex Cells

The sperm cell and the egg have an extra chromosome – the 23rd. It is these 23rd chromosomes when joined together in the fertilized egg that determine the sex of the new baby. Sperm cells decide whether the new body machine will be a boy or girl. Eggs have an extra X chromosome. Some sperms have X and some have an extra Y chromosome. If an X sperm fertilizes an egg, the baby will be a girl. If a Y sperm does it, it will be a boy.

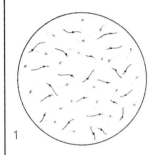

1

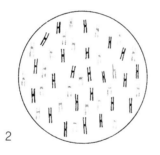

2

(3) Every chromatid from the mother has a matching one from the father, these move together and are called a *bivalent*. There are now 92 chromosomes – 23 sets of 4. The wall of the nucleus now dissolves, the bivalent splits across the middle, and 23 chromatids move to each end of the cell. A new nucleus wall develops around each batch of 23 chromatids. The chromatids split up. Two new cells have been formed with 46 chromosomes identical to (1).

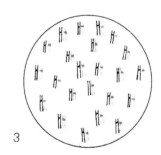

3

(1) This is a cell nucleus just after fertilization. It contains 46 chromosomes – 23 from the sperm and 23 from the egg. In order for the embryo to develop, this cell has to duplicate itself over and over again.

(2) First each of the 46 chromosomes duplicates itself (see diagram opposite) to form 46 pairs of 2 chromosomes. A pair of chromosomes is called a *chromatid*.

(6) Each nucleus wall disappears again, and the 23 chromatids in each cell split up and a new nucleus wall forms around each batch of split chromatids, making 4 nuclei with 23 chromosomes in each. These are now sex cells waiting to join with another sex cell to form another human being.

(4) The sex cells contain only 23 chromosomes, half the number in an ordinary cell nucleus. When stage (3) is reached, instead of a bivalent splitting across the middle – a crossover takes place (shown here is one bivalent crossing over).

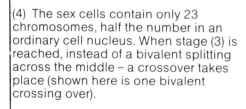

4

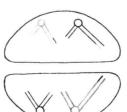

5

(5) Now 23 of these crossed-over chromatids move to each end of the cell as in (3). Remember a chromatid is 2 chromosomes joined together. A new nucleus wall develops round each batch to form two new cells each with 23 chromatids.

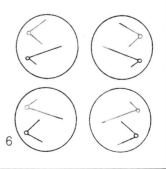

6

HOW YOU SEE THE WORLD

Feedback

Recently robots have been made which can perform tasks without using a human being to control them. Robots have made this step forward because a feedback mechanism has been invented for them. The same mechanism is already found in the body machine. If you are holding an egg, a message about how tightly you are holding the egg is sent back to your brain by the sense of touch in your fingers. If you are squeezing too hard and likely to crush the egg, your brain sends a message to your finger muscles to make them relax. If you are about to drop the egg because your finger muscles have become too relaxed, the brain sends another message to the finger muscles to make them tighten their grip. So feedback makes sure you do not hold the egg too tightly or drop it.

The human body needs to deal with hundreds of different feedbacks at the same time. To do this the body has a number of self-correcting systems which cut in and out as they are needed. When you run you need your heart, lungs and motor muscles. So energy is diverted away from the digestive system. When you are digesting food, more of your energy goes to the

◆ Robots that attack their creators and robots that take over the world only exist in films. Recently robots have been made which use feedback to perform tasks without using a human being to control them. This is still a long way from the robots in science fiction.

◆ If you strap a watch to your wrist, your touch neurons at first register that you are wearing a watch. But after a while you stop feeling it. The brain has switched the sensation off so that your brain can concentrate on something else.

digestive system. So you sometimes feel sleepy after a heavy meal. These cut-outs are like thermostats which turn off the heating when a particular temperature is reached.

The master thermostat is the brain itself. But it does more than simply switch off and on. It is constantly altering the setting at which the thermostat system will switch off and on to take account of changing conditions in the outside world. This is called **feed-forward**.

The brain responds very quickly to sudden sensations and alerts the body. But if the sensations go on for a long time, the brain decides that they are not so important and it tells the body to relax again. You can experience this for yourself. Switch on the radio quite loud and try to talk to somebody in the same room. You will probably have to shout to make yourself heard. If you leave the radio playing for a few minutes, it will not sound so loud and you will probably be able to talk quite normally. Your brain has decided that the radio is part of the background and it doesn't need to take so much notice of it – so the sensation of loudness has lessened.

♠ The feedback mechanism needs only a short time to work properly. But some actions are so fast that there is not enough time for the feedback mechanism to operate. Performing an **arpeggio** – a rapid succession of notes – on the piano is such an action. It has to be planned in advance and then launched like a rocket.

FACTS
People suffering from high blood pressure can reduce it using a combination of yoga or meditation with biofeedback. Your blood pressure is measured and heard as bleeps on a special machine. By concentrating on cutting the frequency of bleeps, you can actually reduce them. This shows that the blood pressure has been lowered.

Memory

Memory is the key to how you see the world. Everything that happens to us is filed away in a special part of the brain called the cerebral cortex. Any action the body machine takes uses information stored there.

> What is yellow outside, grey inside and
> has a wonderful memory?
> *An elephant omelette!*

Without a memory that terrible joke would be gobbledygook – by the time you reached the end of the sentence, you would have forgotten the beginning. So no memory means no fun. Mind you there are people that have such incredible memories that they remember everything whether they want to or not. Not much fun either.

A Russian memory man, called Shereshevskii, could not forget anything and this nearly drove him mad. Just as he was about to go completely crazy, he thought of a way to get rid of some of his memories. He imagined writing whatever he wanted to forget on a blackboard and then imagined rubbing it out. It worked, and he was able to forget everything he wanted to forget.

Most people's memories lie between these two extremes. The brain has an enormous capacity to

♦ Time does odd things to memories. I'm sure you can remember this dramatic event but can you remember in which year it happened? (Answer on page 91.)

FACTS

The longest part in a play was memorized by actor Russell Denton. The play, by Neil Oram, was called 'The Warp' and Mr Denton was on the stage for 18 hours.

The record for the longest joke-telling session from memory belongs to comedian Bob Caroll, who cracked away for 24 hours 5 minutes.

A man in Turkey recited 6666 verses of the Koran, equivalent to a quarter of the Bible, from memory. It took him 6 hours, and he made not a single mistake.

♦ Remembering faces can be difficult. Here are five faces, only one of which is famous. Can you remember his name? What does he do? (Answer on page 91.)

remember. Some scientists say that the brain registers everything and when you can't remember something it is because you are not very good at recalling information from the memory.

People recognize this, and memory joggers are used to help the memory. Posters remind you when a pop concert starts. Signposts remind you of the directions to the sea. Memorials, maps, diaries, calendars, knots in handkerchiefs – every item on this list is to help remind you of something important.

How good a memory do you have?

◆ Forgetting can be an expensive business. In 1974 Japanese railway passengers forgot the following on trains: £75,000 each day (nearly £27 million a year!); 500,000 umbrellas; 400,000 pieces of clothing; 72 pairs of dentures and seven boxes of human ashes.

Test your memory on the following question: where would you expect to find an oasis?

Here is a list of numbers. Speak the first number sequence, cover it and speak it back, then the second line and so on. At some point you will forget a whole line. You will then be able to measure the span of your immediate memory. Test your friends and family. The average number span for your age is given on page 91.

384	962829
4362	4516832
9713	3496579
27381	48823870
74922	706630105
109596	591077384

Do you want to improve your memory? Try saying each number aloud, in blocks of two or three.

● It is important to make sense of what you are seeing. Familiar objects seen in close-up or from an unfamiliar angle are sometimes hard to recognize. Can you guess what this is? (Answer on page 91.)

● It is difficult learning to walk because the part of the brain responsible for coordination and balance, the cerebellum, is still developing. So young children tend to wobble and jerk as they move.

Learning

A very young child will think it cannot be seen when it stands in the middle of a room with its hands over its eyes. Because the child cannot see anyone or anything, it thinks no one can see it. But soon the child will learn by trial and error – by doing it again and again – that this is not so.

As soon as a baby boy or girl is old enough to hold things, it starts to learn by trial and error. A baby will shake everything. After a while, it will find that one of its toys will rattle. The baby will continue to shake things, hoping that it will come across another toy that rattles. Eventually the baby will learn to recognize the toy and know that it will make a noise. Recognizing something as a rattle is the first step to seeing and understanding – *perceiving* things. Soon the baby will be able to predict so easily that its rattle will make a noise that it will become bored with it.

The baby must now be given new toys, otherwise it may lose interest with learning by trial and error.

A baby lying in its cot in the garden recognizes very little when it looks round. Its mother's face, her smell, or perhaps the sound of a pet dog barking. This is not because the baby's senses are not working properly. It is just that the baby cannot perceive (see and understand) as much as its mother.

Soon the baby will begin to make noises, starting with gurgling sounds. The baby will make them in answer to someone talking to it. After a while it will begin to copy very simple sounds like 'Aah'. The first real words will probably be 'Mama' or 'Dada' because those words will have been repeated most often to the baby. Because a baby learns this type of skill by copying, it is important that babies are talked to.

So, if you have a baby brother or sister, make sure you talk to him or her a lot.

How do we learn best? (Answer on page 91.)

◆ Playing is a good way of learning about the world while enjoying yourself. By running about with toy guns, this little boy is improving the habit of using hand and eye together.

FACTS

As an example of how animals learn, make quacking sounds (or any other sound) at a newborn duckling, and it will follow you, instead of its mother, for the rest of its life.

Kim Ung-Yong of South Korea learnt to speak four languages (Korean, English, German and Japanese) at the age of 4 years 8 months. Both his parents are university professors and both were born at 11 a.m. on 23rd May 1934.

65

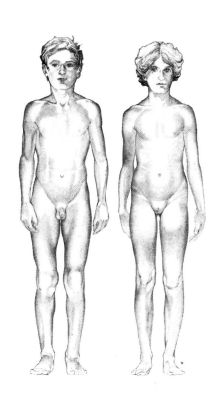

10 – 14   15 – 19

> ♠ Sudden changes occur at puberty in boys and girls.
> *Boys* Jaws become squarer. Hair begins to grow on face, chest, under the arms and around the penis. The penis grows thicker and longer. Muscles develop. Height increases. Shoulders and chest become broader. Voice becomes lower.
> *Girls* Breasts start to develop. Voice gets slightly lower. Hips become broader. Body hair starts to grow. Thighs become rounded. Height increases. Girls also start to menstruate.

Growing Up

From birth onwards, the body machine gradually grows towards a stage where it can make new body machines. For a long time after babyhood, children's bodies keep on growing at a steady rate. But then comes a stage – called **adolescence** – at which very important changes take place.

The physical part of adolescence is called **puberty**. It usually starts at the age of 11 in girls and at 13 in boys. But these ages can vary enormously, and an early or late start makes no difference to how you turn out at the end.

Puberty starts when the pituitary gland in the brain starts to make a new hormone. This hormone tells parts of the body to produce sex hormones. In boys, sex hormones are made by the testicles. In girls, hormones are made by the ovaries. The hormones trigger off the changes you can see in the diagram. After about two years, the most important changes have happened. By now boys have begun to make sperm, and girls have begun to produce eggs that can be fertilized. Adolescents' bodies will continue to grow a little more, but from now on a girl can become pregnant and a boy can become a father.

These physical changes will at times be accompanied by feelings of confusion. Inside your brain, hormones are beginning to prepare your mind and body for life as a grown-up. For example an adolescent may begin to think of how life might feel away from parents and how he or she will cope with it. At school, he or she is expected to be more grown up, and to understand more difficult ideas. To cope with these problems, the adolescent must work out what he or she thinks and what he wants to do. Although this is difficult at first, as time goes on, the mind gets used to grappling with problems and life becomes more fun.

Adolescence marks the end of the assembly line. The body machine is now complete and ready for testing.

What is the first sign of puberty? (Answer on page 91.)

▶ Young teenagers want to be independent, so they dress up in outrageous clothes and wear their hair in odd styles, but they still have some of the unsureness of children, so they clump together in gangs for security.

FACTS

The average child grows 7.5 cm during the first year, 9 cm in the second and 7.5 cm in the third. There is a further 3.1 cm growth the year after and 2 cm in the next. The average adolescent growth spurt reaches a peak by the age of 12 in girls and 14 in boys.

Boys stop growing out of their trousers a year before they grow out of their jackets, because the legs usually grow before the body.

◆ All Jewish boys have a **bar mitzvah** at the age of 13. It is a ritual that marks the change from child to adult. Confirmation in church is another example of a ritual that marks this change.

• Former US president Gerald Ford falls down the steps of an aeroplane. Aeroplanes travel fast enough for us to reach parts of the world where it is still daylight when our body clock is telling us we should be in bed. As a result on arrival the body is often tired out in the middle of the day.

• People like to drink tea or coffee in the morning, because as you warm up, the body starts to work more smoothly. You will not get the best performance from a car if you turn on the engine early on a cold winter's day.

Body Clocks

The body machine has its own clocks – automatic timers which tell your body machine to do certain things at certain times. Feeling sleepy, feeling hungry are just two of the feelings that happen regularly.

To find out how these work, we can take a look at a simpler body machine than our own – that of a swallow. You probably know that towards the end of summer, some birds, like the swallow, take off and fly to warmer parts of the world for the winter. How do they know that winter is coming? A part of the swallow's brain is sensitive to the amount of daylight.

And when the hours of daylight fall to a certain level, the brain automatically triggers off a hormone which lets the bird know that it is time to go.

Inside the human body machine are many clocks like this. Each of them triggers off a hormone at a certain time of day, which makes you behave in a certain way.

At lunchtime, whether lunch is ready or not, a hormone is triggered off which starts the digestive juices squirting. That's why your tummy rumbles at lunchtime. At bedtime, a hormone makes your heartbeat and temperature fall. If, as an experiment, you sat all day and all night in a specially lighted room – without a watch so you didn't know the time – the hormone would still make your heartbeat and temperature fall at your normal bedtime. It is hard to change the clock inside your body machine.

Does the full moon affect our body clocks?

FACTS
Over the last 150 years, the first half of the year has usually seen more births in Great Britain and America than the second half. Since 1840, April to June have always been the most popular months.

● Birds' body clocks are so accurate that birds migrate south at almost the same time every year. They have an internal timer that enables them to judge day length, but we do not know yet how it works.

◆ Although feelings start in the brain, they are closely linked to the body. If something goes wrong when you are tired or hungry, you will feel more angry than if you are relaxed. If you get really angry, you may try to kick whoever is making you feel angry. But this is a bad thing to do and you will probably get into trouble.

Emotions and Feelings

Sometimes you feel happy, and sometimes you feel sad or angry. These feelings are called **emotions**. Everybody has them. Emotions begin with changes that happen deep within the brain. Sometimes these changes take place because of things which happen inside the body. At other times, the changes begin with events in the outside world. Whichever it is, the changes get mixed with the thinking part of the brain and allow you to think, or say, 'I feel happy,' 'I feel sad,' or 'I feel angry'.

All this can happen very quickly indeed. Have you ever been startled by some sudden noise? Can you remember what happened? Your heart suddenly 'jumped', and you felt a tingle all over your body. Afterwards you can say, 'That made me jump' or 'I was startled.' This is a strong reaction. Not all our reactions are so strong. But all of them are closely linked with changes in our body. For instance, if you

FACTS

To discover more about emotions, scientists have experimented on monkeys. Electrodes placed into certain parts of monkeys' brains cause feelings of pleasure to them. This is proved when an electrode that works when a monkey presses a bar replaces an ordinary electrode. Some monkeys press the bar up to 17,000 times in an hour before falling over, exhausted.

are tired or hungry, you may find yourself irritated by things more quickly than usual.

People often speak of the need to *control* emotions. This is because emotions can happen so quickly that you may do something that later you wish you hadn't. So how can you control your feelings? One way is, every time you have a strong feeling, whether good or bad, to try to work out what caused it. If it was a bad feeling, you will know to keep away from such situations in the future. If it was a good feeling, you will know where to look for more good feelings.

Another way is to talk about it with other people. If you can say 'I feel bad because . . .', you are halfway to getting a grip on the feeling. It's as though the thinking part of the brain is helping the feeling part of your brain to slow down a little.

If someone is described as highly emotional, what does it mean?

♠ Babies and young children can only express themselves by laughing or crying. But as you grow older and learn to talk you become calmer and express yourself in a different way. You have begun to understand why you feel the way you do.

♦ Clowns make people laugh, but people don't only laugh when they find something funny. They also laugh if they are nervous and unsure of what to do. If you laugh a lot, people think that you have a happy personality. It does not mean that you feel happy all the time, you will feel all the other emotions, too.

* Charles Manson is in prison for murder. His mind is ill, and doctors say he is a psychopath. Psychopaths tend to be restless, react angrily towards discipline and be cruel to children and animals.

Why do people take personality tests?

Gangs
* Ten year olds are often very uncertain of themselves and form gangs to give them confidence. The members are usually either all boys or all girls. They stick closely together and have a leader, who is often the strongest and cleverest. At the age of 16 or 17, children find gangs less important. They make friends with people of both sexes, who have the same interests. Some people have lots of friends, some choose only a few, but everyone thinks that friends are important.

Do You Like Me?

Babies spend most of their time finding out about the world and getting better at doing things like moving about or eating or drawing. Everybody around them is part of their own secure world. They cannot understand that other people have their own lives to live. Then suddenly, at about the age of three, they become very shy because they no longer feel so secure. Do you remember the first time you felt shy? It may have been the first time you went to a birthday party. If you had this feeling, it was because you wondered whether the other children would let you play with them or whether they would talk to you.

Usually children make friends at school. They play in the playground in groups of boys and girls and have one or two best friends. Then, one day, one friend invites the other home for tea. This first meeting outside school is often difficult. At school people do the same things. There is a routine that everybody shares. But each person's home routine is different. The visiting child may feel a little out of place at first or the other child may be worried that his or her toys are not good enough for the friend or that his house or bedroom isn't very nice. But parents can soon help

◆ Some people are terrified of heights. Fear of something that is not going to harm you is called a **phobia**. Phobias come in all shapes and sizes. For instance, children are often afraid of the dark. Other phobias are: fire, lightning, madness, dirt, hair, snakes, spiders, cats, mice, birds, open spaces and closed spaces. Fear of flowers, water and numbers are rarer.

them both to adjust, and ten mintes after the friend arrives it's as if they were playing at school.

It is very important to adjust, because everybody has a different way of behaving, or of reacting to things. The differences add up to something called **personality** – the habits and ways of looking at the world which go to make you the person you are. As you get older the more your way of doing things becomes different from other people's. You'll need to adjust to the way they do things, just as they'll have to adjust to the way you do things. At the same time you'll also find yourself making friends with people who like many of the things that you yourself do.

FACTS
Between the ages of about 7 and 12, children prefer to play only with other children of the same sex.

Personality tests ask questions like: Someone you have just met says nice things about you. Do you
a) feel embarrassed?
b) feel suspicious?
c) feel flattered and start to like him?
All those who answer yes to (a) find it difficult to express themselves. Those who answered yes to (b) are very cold. Those who answered yes to (c) express themselves freely – but not unwisely.

◆ Nowadays special doctors called psychiatrists try to cure people who have problems. They get the patient to talk about his or her problems and bring them out in the open, so that the doctor and the patient can deal with them. If the problems stay inside the mind, they can become frightening and do harm.

Words and Signs

You have seen how you talk and how babies learn to talk, but why do you talk?

The complexity of the human brain allows us to work out problems and see how things work. But humans also need to share, or communicate, needs, feelings, problems and solutions for many reasons.

From an early age we need to communicate. When your parents are woken in the middle of the night by the cries of your baby brother or sister, they probably don't seem very happy. But this is just the baby communicating the fact that he or she is hungry or upset. Later, people need to be able to share their thoughts and actions, partly because ten people can do more than one. Speech is the main way of doing this. It also allows us to express our own personalities, to talk about problems and agree on solutions.

The words that we use to talk or write to each other are known as **language**. The English language, for instance, has about half a million different words. A child just starting school doesn't know many words, between 1200 and 2000, but as we grow older we learn from other people and from books more and more ways of saying things. The vocabulary of an average university student is said to be 25,000 words.

Language need not only be words. We can communicate through sign language and body language, which is showing how you feel by the way you stand and move. If you are in a country where you don't speak the language and you want to have a drink, you can pretend to bring a cup to your lips. You will then be directed to the nearest drinking place – unless you are in a country where pretending to bring a cup to your lips is a rude sign! Deaf and dumb people learn their own sign language, which allows them to express what they feel quite rapidly.

On the whole, however, sign language and body language are not clear enough by themselves to communicate clearly and quickly. But next time you watch two or three people talking together, notice how they use gestures and body language.

What is a cleft palate? (Answer on page 91.)

♠ Without speech these airmen would be unable to pass on or receive information. As a result, the plane would almost certainly crash into something, because the navigator would not be able to tell the pilot which way to go.

Signs

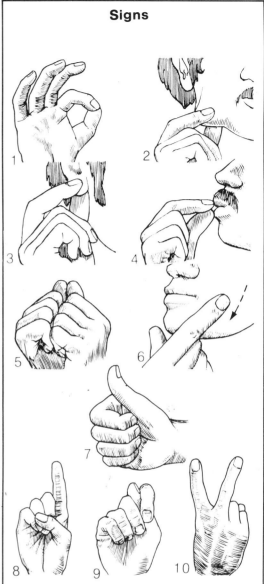

Gestures are an important part of communication. 1–7 are all gestures showing approval. (1) 'Wonderful' in USA, Europe and Iran. 'Beautiful' in Italy. (2) 'Wonderful' in Sicily. (3) 'Wonderful' in Brazil. (4) 'Beautiful' in France. (5) 'What a beautiful girl' in Brazil. (6) 'Hello, beautiful' in Spain and Portugal. (7) 'Great' in Great Britain. Sometimes gestures of approval in one place are insults in another. (8) is 'Good Luck' in Brazil, but an insult in the USA. (9) is 'I've got an idea' in Italy, Austria and among Jews, but an insult to most people in the USA and Great Britain. (10) is very rude in Great Britain but means 'V for Victory' in South America.

Dreaming

♦ When you are dreaming your eyes dart about rapidly and your muscles relax. Scientists think that dreaming is a way of sorting out and reacting to events in our waking life. In any case, dreaming is essential. Repeatedly waking someone up as they are about to start dreaming will make them very unsettled.

FACTS

Girls sleep more soundly than boys.

About 350 g in weight are lost during sleep each night.

The longest period someone has gone without sleep is 14 days 13 hours.

In 1888 a 15-year-old girl yawned continuously for 5 weeks.

KEEPING FIT

Sleep Tight

The body cannot be driven flat out all the time, 24 hours a day. It needs 7 to 10 hours each day to recover its energy.

The body does not switch off completely though or we should never wake up. The brain remains extremely active, and it is the muscles that take a rest and the heart that slows down.

How much sleep do you need? There are no rules, but about one third of our life is spent asleep, so by

♠ A newborn baby sleeps about 16 hours a day. But a 12-year-old boy needs only about 9 hours.

● When your body is tired it tries to take in more oxygen to liven it up. Yawning allows more air to enter the body. You have probably noticed that you yawn when in a stuffy room. This is also because of the lack of fresh air. Yawning is infectious, if one person starts, the people nearby will soon follow.

the time you are 60 you will have slept for 20 years. Although some people need more sleep than others, an average adult sleeps for 7 hours 20 minutes in a 24-hour period.

There are two types of sleep: deep sleep and dream sleep. Most of the night you are in a deep sleep, but about five times a night you will dream for a period lasting anything from 10 to 30 minutes (see box).

Do you know anyone who walks in their sleep? Children are twice as likely to be sleepwalkers as adults. They are usually in only a light sleep. Their eyes may even be open. Recently a 14-year-old girl fell 5 m from a window into her garden. Amazingly, she stayed asleep despite a broken foot and severe scratches from a rose bush which helped to break her fall. Sleeptalking is much more common. Sometimes people sit up in bed and shout. Mostly they talk complete nonsense!

● Another way to relieve a tired mind is by meditation. This man is in a state of deep rest while being completely alert. He is just on the verge of sleep. Many of the physical changes in your body during meditation are similar to those that occur during sleep. To achieve this state takes years of practice.

● During a night's sleep you change position about 40 times. Each movement takes about 30 seconds. If you snore you will snore between movements. The only cure for snoring is to wake the snorer up.

What is the longest dream ever recorded?

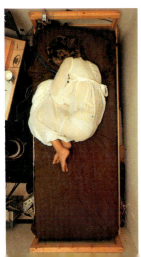

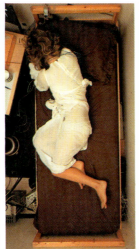
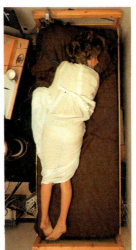

What Do You Eat?

This table shows how many calories are needed every day for a junior body machine:

Age	Calories
0-1	800
1-2	1200
2-3	1400
3-5	1600
5-7	1800
7-9	2100
9-12	2400
12-15	2600
15-18	2700

What you eat is called your diet. Between the ages of seven and sixteen, you can eat a moderate amount of junk food, provided the other things you eat are reasonably healthy. That means not too much fat (butter, ice cream), plenty of starch (potatoes) and fibre (baked beans), wholemeal bread, and not too much meat. After this age, people are more likely to get fat and so have to watch what they eat. Try varying your diet too.

Food gives the body machine the energy it needs to maintain itself whether at rest or in action. We have already seen that food is broken down into energy-

● Too many carrots? It would be hard to take too much Vitamin A which is found in carrots, but a man once drank so much carrot juice that he is reported to have turned yellow and died. So vary your diet!

● Fatness or obesity is a disease of the richer nations and is usually caused by overeating. Not only does it not look very nice, it can also lead to high blood pressure, heart disease and arthritis.

This table shows how many calories are in different foods.

Food	Average portion	Calories
Apple	2	140
Bacon	2 rashers	250–320
Banana	1	110
Beef	200 g steak	388
Bread (wholemeal)	3 slices	241
Butter	for 1 slice	110
Cabbage (boiled)	110 g	15
Cheese (cheddar)	100g	410
Chips	170 g	270
Milk chocolate	100 g	578
Corn flakes	1 bowl	100
Egg (boiled)	1	90
Milk	cup	110
Orange	1	60
Peanuts	110 g	330
Rice (boiled)	110 g	600
Sardines (tinned)	4 fish	240
Sausages (pork)	2	400
Sugar	1 teaspoon	25
Tea	cup	15
Tomato	1	12

giving chemicals which are transported by the blood to the cells, where it explodes with oxygen to give energy. Just as a certain amount of coal in a furnace gives a certain amount of heat, so a certain amount of food makes a certain amount of energy. Energy is measured in calories. The amount of calories a junior body machine needs is listed in the table (left). Even when the body is asleep, it needs about one-sixth of its total intake of calories every day just to tick over. To give you some idea of what a calorie is worth, there is a list of foods above with their calorific values.

The wrong kind of diet can harm the body. Too much sugar rots teeth, so it is important to clean them regularly. Jelly, biscuits, cakes and sweets, as well as tomatoes and many frozen foods all contain a great deal of sugar – the trouble is they taste so good!

What is a calorie? (Answer on page 91.)

◆ Any fat not digested in the intestines is transported around the body as tiny droplets in the blood. If you eat too much fat, the fat that is not needed starts to coat the walls of the major arteries. This puts strain on the heart, which may eventually break down.

FACTS

In a lifetime we consume 50 tonnes of food and 50,000 litres of liquid. Among other substances, the body contains enough fat for seven cakes of soap, enough lime to whitewash a small shed, enough phosphorus to make 2200 matches, as much iron as there is in a small nail and as much carbon as would be found in a bag of coke weighing 11 kg.

Exercise

If a car is left in the garage for a long time, it may not start first time. Even if it does, it may splutter and spurt until all the dirt has been blown out of its system and it is moving smoothly. In the same way, if you allow your body to sit around it will become stiff and awkward. It is very important to take regular exercise.

Exercise tunes up the muscles, especially the heart muscle, and gets all the body systems moving more smoothly. It's a way of making the body machine

FACTS

Here are a few exercises for you to do. But remember if you feel tired, you have probably had enough. Don't overdo it.

(1) **Side bends** Press the hands down alternate sides bending at the waist.

(2) **Half-squats** Bend the knees to a semi-sitting position while extending the arms horizontally. Return to the original position.

(3) **Sit-ups** Lying on your back, rise to a semi-sitting position, until your hands reach your knees. Slowly return to your original position.

(4) **Back exercise** Lying face down, clasp your hands behind your back and raise your chest and legs from the ground.

(5) **Spot running** Run on the spot for 20 strides, then do a half-squat.

♦ There is no doubt that exercise is good for you. But many doctors think that it is possible to overdo exercise. For a grown-up, an hour or so of regular exercise a week is enough to keep the body machine healthy all through its life.

capable of more work with less feeling of effort. And because your mind and body are linked in so many ways, being fit makes you feel better as well.

Keeping fit is not something the junior body machine normally has to worry about very much. It has a lot of natural energy, and most young people do enough running about to stay fit and supple. But for older people it is more important.

Without exercise a person aged 60 may behave as a 70 year old. Scientists have shown that people aged 80 or more have a much clearer mind if they have led a life full of exercise than if they had spent their life not looking after themselves. Fit 80 year olds are also much less likely to get sick.

In the last ten years, more and more people have come to realize that fitness is a good thing. The streets and parks are full of joggers, and there are regular marathon runs in which hundreds of people take part.

Many doctors think it is possible to overdo exercise. Junior body machines are still growing into their full strength, so it pays to be sensible about the amount of exercise you do over and above your normal activity. If you want to know more, it is best to ask the advice of your school sports instructor.

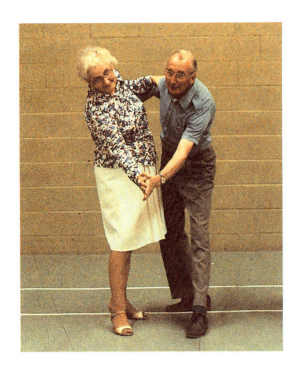

♠ Seventy-year-olds exercising in a dance class. One of many ways of keeping fit, this kind of energy follows on from an active adult life. An alert mind in old age is also more likely if you have led an active life.

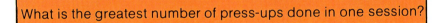

What is the greatest number of press-ups done in one session?

♦ City children are usually taller and grow more quickly than children who live in country villages. This may be because country children burn up more energy in running around than town children, as well as consuming less energy-giving food.

Hair is lost
Hair becomes grey or white
Hearing becomes poorer
Eyesight becomes poorer
Teeth are lost
Skin wrinkles
Muscles sag
Joints stiffen

Nose bulges out more
Top layer of skin thins out, so blood vessels stand out
Freckles appear on the back of the hands
Hand grip weakens
Height decreases slightly

The Old Bits

As you grow old the heart and lungs don't work like they used to. Loss of memory and other signs of mental weakening occur as the brain cells die. Old people are sometimes confused and forgetful and cannot look after themselves. But only about one old person in ten becomes like this.

FACTS

The oldest proven human of all-time is Shigechiyo Izumi of Japan who was 118 on 29th June 1983.

The oldest recorded mother was a Mrs Kistler who gave birth to a healthy daughter when she was 57 years 129 days old.

The average lifespan of Europeans and Americans is 71 years.

Getting Old

The body machine is designed to reach its peak at the age of 20 or so, ready to have children when you are at your most energetic. After that the body gets older and does not work so well. But nowadays it is less usual for people aged 20 to settle down and have children. Many people want to get a good job or travel before they settle down and become responsible for a family.

Some parts of the body get older quicker than others. Pads of cartilage grow between bones causing stiffness in the joints and making it harder to walk, all the senses become less sensitive, muscles sag and nerve cells die, bones break more easily, and skin dries out. The circulation of the blood gets worse, so the brain gets less oxygen and does not work as well. But it takes many years for these signs to show and many more before function is affected. It is possible, to some extent, to slow the ageing process down. Some of the signs we associate with old age —stooping posture and a wobbly walk – are due more to lack of regular exercise than to the ageing process.

As you have seen, although we can describe how we age, nobody knows why it happens. Some scientists believe that after a certain age some cells have divided so many times that they can no longer reproduce themselves exactly (see page 58) and they don't work properly. Other scientists believe that the body's defence mechanism changes dramatically after a certain age and starts to destroy itself rather than invading germs.

Incidentally nobody dies of old age. There is always a reason why people die. The heart and lungs do not stop working on their own. Something has to make them stop, either disease or shock.

How old is old? If you are an athlete 20 is old. If you are a footballer 35 is old. If you are a politician 40 is young. If you are a child star 16 is old. And if you are a grandmother 50 is young. So oldness depends on how you compare to other people doing the same thing. Which is which? Answers on page 91.

What are the three main causes of death?

Your Health

● This man is getting away from it all for a spot of quiet fishing. The more you relax and rest the healthier you will be. A life free of tension and anxiety will be a longer and better one.

You now know that your body machine is very complicated. Many systems and many moving parts all work together. And for most of the time, things work miraculously well. In this book, most of the descriptions of the junior body machine have assumed that the machine is in perfect working order. But, of course, things can go wrong and most people become ill at one time or another. Most of the time the body machine puts itself right. When it can't, doctors are on hand to help.

The main things that go wrong with the body machine are caused by disease, breakdown or injury. Unfortunately, like many new machines off the production line, a few of us are born with faults – a squint or even a hole in the heart. Many of these faults can be put right in hospital.

Some diseases are prevented because you have special chemical soldiers in your body which fight a

specific disease (see page 89). When you are very young, you don't have any of these special soldiers and so you are almost bound to get one of the illnesses that almost all children get – measles, chickenpox or mumps. If you had caught these diseases a hundred years ago, you might have died, but modern advances in medicine mean that almost everyone is cured soon after falling ill.

Once out of childhood, the average grown-up is fairly safe from disease, except for minor illnesses. As long as you keep fit you have a 90 per cent chance of recovering from most diseases, even if you never see a doctor in your life.

Calmness and relaxation are important, too. If you worry too much or work too hard, you are more likely to be ill.

What is the Red Cross? (Answer on page 91.)

- Don't worry if you spend a week in bed with a bug. All children get ill early on, before they have built up a protection (immunity) from all the germs in the air. Just remember you have a 90 per cent chance of recovering from most diseases without ever needing to see a doctor.

- One way that the body can go wrong is through injury. This footballer has injured his knee quite badly. He certainly will not be able to play any football for a bit.

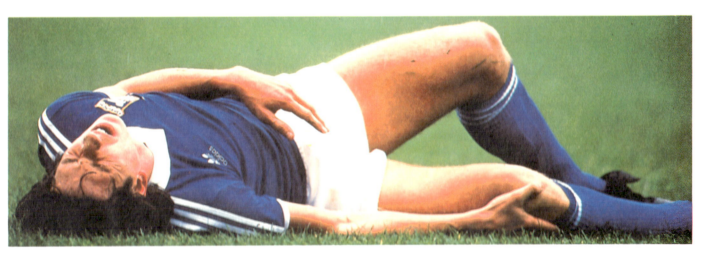

Going to Hospital

Had your tonsils out? These children are all recovering from minor operations like that. They are allowed out of bed to play so long as they do not get under the feet of the busy nurses.

FACTS

The District Medical Center in Chicago USA has a total of 5600 beds.

In remote parts of the world, like Australia, doctors travel huge distances by aeroplane to tend the sick. They are called Flying Doctors.

The busiest maternity hospital is in Zaire. 41,930 babies were born in 1976.

Going to hospital is like taking a car to the repair shop. It happens when a part of your body machine needs mending. Hospitals are places where experts – doctors and nurses – can have the space and the equipment they need to work on the body machine. A person may not go into hospital more than two or three times in his or her life. But there are so many people in the world that hospitals work 24 hours a day. Nearly all parts of a hospital are busy, but one place that gets especially busy is the Accident Department. If somebody has a bad accident or suddenly becomes very ill, he or she will be whisked off in an ambulance to the casualty unit of the local hospital. There a team of doctors and nurses will be standing-by ready to start repairing the damage. If the damage is bad, an operation may be necessary. In that case the patient will be taken to an operating theatre. Before operating they may take the patient to the **radiology** department. In this department they have a special camera which takes photographs, called X-rays, of the inside of the body.

Preventing Illness

Of course, hospitals would rather everybody was healthy and that all their beds were empty. As you probably realize, this will never happen. In fact, hospitals now try to persuade people to come and have regular check-ups to make sure that nothing is wrong. Hospitals can also give advice on how to stay healthy in everyday life.

If you ever have to go to hospital, for whatever reason, you will be put to bed in a ward. Doctors will carry out tests to try to find out what is wrong. When they find out what it is, the nurse will come and give you whatever medicine you need to get better.

Where was the first hospital and when was it founded?

● Doctors make up only a small part of the total staff of a hospital. There are cleaners and cooks, porters and nurses. Nurses see to the day-to-day care of the patients and work very hard.

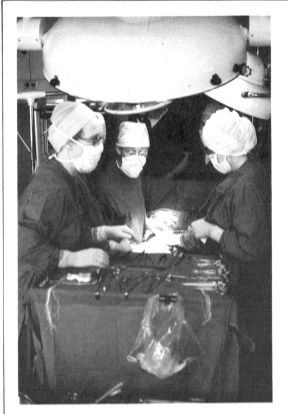

Right Amputation instruments c. 1840. Hospitals are much better than they used to be, and instruments like these rarely have to be used.

The Operating Theatre

Operations are sometimes necessary to mend the body. These are carried out by surgeons – specially trained doctors who are expert at removing or repairing damaged parts of people's bodies. Some operations, such as removing an appendix, are very simple. But, in the last twenty years, operations have become much more complicated. Giving a patient new kidneys is now quite a common operation. Doctors hope to be able to give patients new livers in the future.

The operating theatre is made sterile – germ free – before the operation begins. The surgeon and his assistants are wearing masks to catch any germs they may breathe out. This keeps the person who is being looked after by the doctors, the patient, safe from infection.

The Blood's Draining System

Subclavian vein

Lymph duct

Lymph node

The body's second circulatory system is the lymphatic system. This runs throughout the body picking up waste fluid that has passed out of the blood vessels and is lying around the nearby tissues. The lymphatic system absorbs this waste fluid, called lymph, and returns it to the bloodstream along two lymphatic ducts emptying into the two subclavian veins near the heart. On its way there, the lymph passes through lymph nodes which pick out and destroy the bacteria, germs and poisons which have been collected. Muscle movement squeezes the lymph vessels, directing the lymph towards the ducts.

The Body's Defences

As you play and run about it may be difficult to imagine that the body needs defending at all. But without the body's defence systems, it would only be a matter of hours before germs and bacteria inside our bodies started to eat away the tissues.

There are three ways that unwanted bacteria and germs can enter the body – through a wound in the skin, by breathing them in and by taking them in with food. Germs are very tough, and to make it as difficult as possible for them to do any harm to your body, there are three lines of defence.

The first line of defence tries to stop bacteria from even getting in to the body. The skin does this job. At the body's openings, like the ears and nose, the skin has been specially made, so that it can secrete, or squirt out, a special sticky liquid called **mucus**, which traps bacteria and dust.

If the skin is cut and bacteria does enter the body, the white blood cells in the **lymph system**, called **phagocytes**, are the second line of defence. They destroy the bacteria preventing them from entering the bloodstream (see diagram).

If the lymph system fails to filter out the bacteria and they enter the bloodstream, the body has a third line of defence. Blood with the bacteria flows into the spleen. The spleen extracts the bacteria, which are destroyed by the millions of phagocytes in the spleen waiting to pounce. Bacteria taken into the body via

FACTS

A child can produce about 100,000 different kinds of antibodies.

A child's spleen is about 75 mm long and lies on the left side of the body, just behind the stomach.

Red blood cells outnumber white blood cells by 700 to 1.

the mouth are usually destroyed by the acid and by enzymes in the stomach and intestines. If the bacteria survive these chemicals and are absorbed into the bloodstream, then as the blood passes through the liver, special cells destroy them there.

This system of traps and filters is backed up by a chemical system known as the **immune response**. This consists of other white blood cells, called **lymphocytes**, which are always in the blood. These fight germs by producing **antibodies**, which make them harmless. Each antibody can fight just one germ. If a germ X enters the body and an antibody X destroys it, the body is said to be immune to germ X.

What do your tonsils and adenoids do? (Answer on page 91.)

◆ Phagocytes are white blood cells which are part of the lymph system and are manufactured in the bone marrow like the red blood cells. Their job is to destroy any germs, bacteria or other unwanted particles in the body. Many white blood cells die in the fight and when the numbers of white blood cells build up, pus is formed.

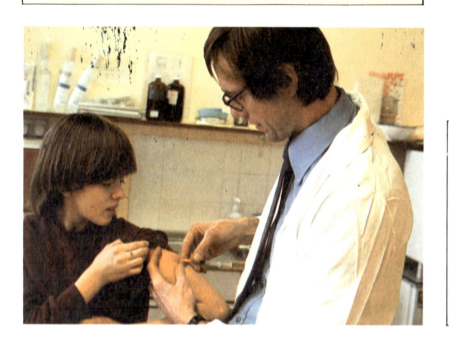

◆ This girl is being vaccinated against measles. This means she is given a tiny dose of the measles germ. The body then produces an antibody to destroy it, which protects the body from the measles germ. This protection is called immunity. Vaccinations are usually given to young children to give them immunity at the earliest possible age.

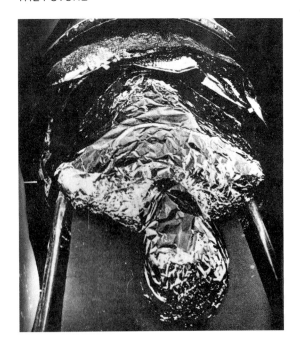

• This dead man or woman will have asked to be stored in a deep freeze after death. He or she will be stored at −190°C, awaiting the moment doctors discover how to revive a corpse!

By the end of the twentieth century, many more advances will have been made. It is thought that:

To make blind people see again, it will be possible to implant tiny TV cameras into the eye and house the electronics in spectacle frames.

Your breakfast will be in the form of a pill which will not only contain a balanced diet but will also taste delicious.

You will be able to spread a bandage on which will heal cuts and grazes very quickly.

At the dentist, an injection will be given against tooth decay and if any decay does start, it can be removed by a spray. No more fillings!

Artificial limbs will be invented that are not only fully manoeuvrable but will also have a sense of touch.

The Future

For centuries scientists have tried to discover the secret of eternal life – of living forever. But built into every cell is a complete story – a beginning, a middle and an end, and so far no scientist has succeeded in changing that.

The long search for immortality has produced some surprising theories. A lot of time has been spent on studying the science of deep-freezing the body – **cryogenics**. The idea being that when somebody becomes ill with an incurable disease, they are preserved alive in a deep-freeze until a cure has been discovered. Some people have paid large sums of money to be deep frozen after death, in the belief that some day it will be possible to revive a corpse!

One of the areas of great advance has been in the field of organ transplants – the practice of exchanging diseased organs for healthy ones, using surgery. Kidney transplants, skin grafts and grafting a new cornea to the eye are already well-established operations with a good success rate. Doctors are working on improving chances of success in transplanting other organs, such as the liver, lungs and pancreas. One problem is that the body can recognize an organ transplanted from another person as not being its own and reject it.

An alternative to transplant surgery is 'spare-part' surgery. Faulty bits of the body are replaced with bits made of metal and plastic. It is estimated that within ten years, hearts made of metal and plastic will routinely be used.

As we move into the twenty-first century, our chances of staying healthy will be much improved

Answers

p. 13 A thin film of epithelial (skin) cells covering internal parts of the body.

p. 15 6 times a minute at night, at least 10 times a minute in the day.

p. 17 The unused part of the digestive system.

p. 19 A storage tank for urine, which enters it from the kidneys along the ureter. It holds about ¼ litre of urine before the urge to empty it affects us.

p. 21 About the size of a man's fist.

p. 23 1.5 litres of blood.

p. 25 Cells of the intestine live only a few days, bone cells may last as long as 30 years, and some neurons last your whole life.

p. 27 About 14 per cent of your total body weight, so the bones of a 31 kg child will weigh 4.5 kg.

p. 29 Your collar bone – between the ages of 18 and 25.

p. 31 It connects your calf muscle to your heel.

p. 33 1.5 square metres.

p. 35 10,000 million neurons.

p. 37 The thicker the nerve, the faster the message. The fastest message travels at 523 km/h, the slowest 2.4 km/h.

p. 39 Paul Anderson lifted 2 844 kg in 1957. The world's most powerful crane has lifted 3000 tonnes (3 million kilograms).

p. 41 At puberty, muscles develop. Since puberty occurs earlier in girls than boys, for a short time girls have more muscle than boys.

p. 43 On the amount of electric power that would light a 10-watt light bulb.

p. 45 A pigment in the cone cells which is gradually eaten away by light during the course of a day and replaced at night. Seeing red or green in front of your eyes after looking at the sun indicates a temporary shortage of visual purple.

p. 47 Not very well. Our smell receptors cover an area of about 1 square centimetre. A dog's receptors cover 100 times that area.

p. 49 Sound travels faster through the ground than through the air, so you can hear sounds travelling through the ground before you can hear them through the air.

p. 51 3 metres of blood vessels, 600 pain sensors, 30 hairs, 300 sweat glands, 4 oil glands, 13 metres of nerves, 9000 nerve endings, 6 cold sensors, 36 heat sensors, 75 pressure sensors.

p. 53 From a Greek word meaning to 'urge on', because hormones urge the body to act in a certain way.

p. 55 0.005 mm.

p. 57 A baby that is lighter than 2.5 kg at birth. They have less chance of survival than a baby born above that weight.

p. 58 Mongol children are not as intelligent as normal children and they look different. Normal cells have 46 chromosomes, the cells of a mongol have 47 chromosomes.

p. 62 The fourth picture is of Clint Eastwood, the American film star.
US President Reagan was shot at in 1981.

p. 63 In a desert.
Average digit span is 2, 3, 4, 5 and 6 digits at the ages of 2½, 3, 4½, 7 and 10 respectively. A university student averages 8 to 9 digits.

p. 64 The heads of some nails.

p. 65 When what you are learning is interesting; by taking short breaks every half an hour; not trying to study immediately after a heavy meal.

p. 67 In boys the testicles start to grow. In girls the breasts start to develop.

p. 69 There is no real proof, but in America statistics show an increase in violent crime at full moon.

p. 71 It means you have a tendency to let emotions get the better of you. You find it difficult to control yourself.

p. 72 Mostly for fun. But it can help to know what sort of personality you have, so that you can improve it if you want to.

p. 75 When a child is born with a split in the roof of its mouth preventing it from eating or talking properly.

p. 77 2 hours 33 minutes. Dream sleep is characterized by rapid eye movements, so it is possible to measure the length of a dream in special sleep laboratories.

p. 79 A unit of heat used to express the amount of energy in a body, so that if you eat a food that has 50 calories, that means that it has given your body fuel which when burned will release 50 calories of energy.

p. 81 9105 by Tommy Gilbert in 1979.

p. 83 Heart disease, cancer and strokes. Starting from the right going clockwise: Sir Stanley Matthews, footballer; David Steel, politician; Mickey Rooney and Judy Garland, child stars; unknown; unknown.

p. 85 A medical organization which aims to relieve suffering of the victims of war and natural disasters.

p. 87 The first hospitals were in Athens in the 7th century BC.

p. 89 They are part of the lymph system that traps germs and bacteria entering the body through the nose and mouth.

Index

Entry numbers in **bold** denote major subjects.
Entry numbers in *italic* refer to boxed panels.